QUILTWEAR

QUILTWEAR
CATHY JOHNSON

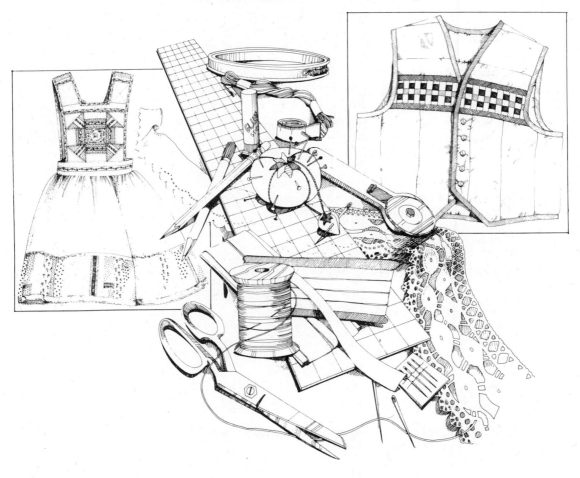

VNR VAN NOSTRAND REINHOLD COMPANY

To designers and patient friends
To my editors, Susan and David
To Roberta, with her great memory and helpful suggestions
To Ruby, for her support and encouragement
To Joe
To Donna, for inspiration
To Molly, Rachel, Nora, and their Dad
To my "fur children," who kept my lap warm and my sense of
humor intact
But mostly to Harris, for everything from proofreading to holding
my hand when the going got rough, from washing dishes to cut-
ting fabric, from posing to lugging props, and for still being
married after all of this

Copyright © 1984 by Van Nostrand Reinhold Company Inc.

Library of Congress Catalog Card Number 84–3631

ISBN 0-442-24351-0

Printed in the United States of America

Designed by Mary McBride

Published by Van Nostrand Reinhold Company Inc.
135 West 50th Street
New York, New York 10020

Van Nostrand Reinhold Company Limited
Molly Millars Lane
Wokingham, Berkshire RG11 2PY, England

Van Nostrand Reinhold
480 La Trobe Street
Melbourne, Victoria 3000, Australia

Macmillan of Canada
Division of Gage Publishing Limited
164 Commander Boulevard
Agincourt, Ontario M1S 3C7, Canada

16 15 14 13 12 11 10 9 8 7 6 5 4 3 2 1

Library of Congress Cataloging in Publication Data
Johnson, Cathy (Cathy A.)
  Quiltwear.

  Bibliography: p. 150
  Includes index.
  1. Clothing and dress. 2. Quilting. I. Title.
TT560.J64 1984   746.9′2   84–3631
ISBN 0-442-24351-0

CONTENTS

INTRODUCTION

The eighties may go down as the decade in which many of us took a hard look at soaring utility bills, turned down the thermostat, and resolved to *do something*. Some people superinsulated their homes, some opted for solar heat, some installed woodburning stoves. But some decided to conserve that most basic of heat sources, our own body heat. We resolved to warm ourselves rather than our surroundings. A national magazine even carried a story on a couple who invested a few hundred dollars in down-quilted clothing, turned their thermostats below 50°, and managed quite comfortably, thank you.

Buying readymade quilted clothing is a perfect answer to a chilly problem; but it can be expensive, and it can look like a "cookie-cutter" uniform. Who wants to look like just another color photo in the Eddie Bauer catalog? Many down or polyfil garments, though practical, make the wearer look like a giant teddy bear. They are hardly flattering and not very individual.

There is an answer that will satisfy even the most discerning tastes. The home-quilted garments contained in the pages of *Quiltwear* are relatively inexpensive, practical, warm, and beautiful. The technique in this book is easy enough for anyone to master. Step-by-step line drawings illustrate the construction methods clearly and simply. I have made these garments myself, and they are worn by friends and family happily *and* cozily. We know they work to keep the thermostat down to a more cost-effective level, and we feel good wearing them, indoors and out.

There is nothing new and revolutionary about quilted clothing, though to look only at the proliferation of down jackets and vests in the last twenty years, you would certainly think a breakthrough had only recently been made. On the contrary, quilting goes back as far as our earliest recorded history, about 5000 B.C., and probably further. Our ancestors were apparently practical sorts. Quilting was not used solely as decoration; it was incorporated into warm clothing as well. The British Museum has a statue of an Egyptian Pharaoh who lived about 3400 B.C.; King Menes is clad in a beautifully quilted jacket, one of the first known examples of quilted clothing.

The Egyptians made use of quilting in many ways. The pattern we know today as Log Cabin is associated in our minds with our pioneer forebears, but it goes much further back than that. In fact, it was used as a design on burial cloths dating before the time of Christ.

The Chinese have known the benefits of well-padded garments for centuries. The quilted cottons of the peasants and the padded and intricately embroidered silks of the nobility both served to ward off the chill Mongolian winds with utility and beauty.

Quilting has never really fallen from favor for long. In the Middle Ages, royalty and peasantry alike kept the art alive. Before the turn of the twentieth century, fine handstitching and beautiful quilting were accomplishments all young women were expected to master. In ancient Egyptian times it was often the men who created quilted garments. In recent history needlework took on a definite feminine bias. But the tide seems to be turning again, as more and more men are beginning to work with fabric and thread.

At a recent showing at the Kansas City Museum of History and Science, quilted bed-coverings were interspersed with hand-quilted garments that we would do well to emulate for warmth *and* beauty. A baby's bonnet with a quilted brim would keep tiny ears snug. Quilted silk petticoats with wool or cotton batting would have kept the cold from great-grandma's knees, but they are striking enough to be worn as outer garments. In fact, modern pattern books are beginning to include skirts with deep quilted borders that echo these early undergarments. A man's vest in the museum collection features an all-over clamshell quilted pattern with handwork so fine that the shells are only a quarter of an inch high and the stitches virtually invisible.

The period between the end of the Great Depression and the burgeoning renaissance of craftsmanship in the sixties was a dry one for quilting. A few women kept the craft alive in mountain cabins and city apartments, and a few daily newspapers continued to feature quilt patterns through the fifties. But the late sixties brought a new interest in all the hand crafts and a revival of interest in our heritage, as well. A healthy skepticism for the dictates of designers in Paris and New York and Tokyo developed as people began to dress more individually, to combine their interest in crafts and clothing and creativity. It was inevitable that patchwork and quilting would escape the bedroom and cedar chest and find their way onto our backs. Perhaps the dictum, "form follows function" applies here as well—the real beauty of usefulness comes into its own.

There are two ways of dealing with realities like high utilities, dwindling resources, and cold homes: we can moan about the hard knocks life has dealt us, or we can create something new and beautiful in answer to our need. *Quiltwear* is like other books on quilted clothing in that it includes basics like sewing and designing. But I have tried to go a step further and make it a practical, helpful, "how-to" book that never loses sight of the ideal balance between beauty and usefulness, between need and creativity.

How to Use This Book

Quiltwear is organized roughly in order of difficulty; that is, easier projects open the book, leading the beginning quilter to the more ambitious projects. Many of the steps in the earlier chapters will be used and reused later in the book, so you may wish to look through the simpler ones even if you have no plans to make a dog coat or man's vest.

The *Beginnings* chapter serves as a general reminder of sewing tips, fabric, and batting information. It covers basic sewing techniques as well as an introduction to string quilting and Seminole patchwork. Look through it for seam finishes, cutting hints, and so forth, but read relevant sections before starting work on a project— cross-references will be provided in each of the projects. For example, some projects call for homemade bias tape to match your project fabric. The *Beginnings* chapter has a section on cutting your own, and it will be suggested that you review the diagrams given there.

At the end of *Quiltwear* I have included a list of Sourcebooks.

This bibliography will provide you with additional reading on related subjects and should be a gold mine of ideas to start you on your way, happily designing your *own* projects. Included are other books on quilted clothes, ethnic designs, and even a booklet on North American Indian footwear. Patchwork designs and quilting ideas can be found here too.

You will find a list of resources at the end of the book. It is intended to put you in touch with mail order sources of fabrics, kits, patterns, and supplies that may not be easily available in your area.

Each projects chapter contains a section at the end called *The Personal Touch*. When I designed the projects for *Quiltwear* and provided step-by-step instructions, I hoped to make it easy for you to reproduce them using, of course, your own favorite patchwork patterns and color combinations. But why stop there? *The Personal Touch* is intended to show different ways to create projects with a similar starting point: idea starters, new directions. You may want to create a garment just like mine, but then again, you may not. Do not feel bound by the ideas shown. Try your own wings and design your own one-of-a-kind quiltwear.

BEGINNINGS

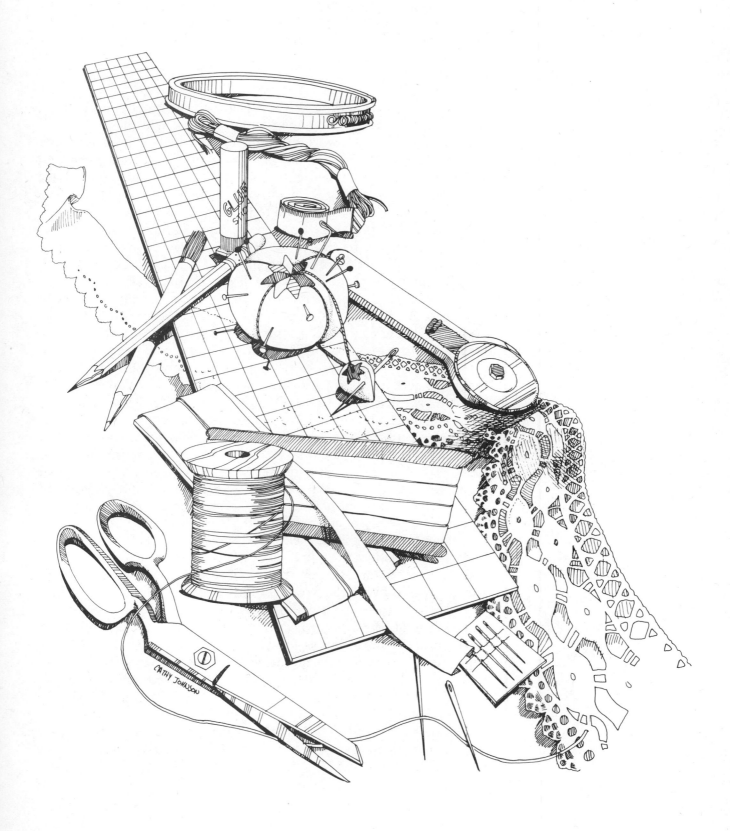

This is a chapter on the basics: choosing fabric for content, color, and pattern; piecing it together; stitching a garment; quilting it; and finishing it. The wide range of battings are compared, and techniques for their use are suggested. Such widely differing subjects as seam finishes, sewing machine care and clothing design can be found in *Beginnings*.

The instructions in this chapter are general, and you will already be familiar with most of this information if you have done any sewing at all. But we can always use a refresher or a new tip. Take the time to remind yourself of these techniques.

Fabric

Most basic to any sewing project is fabric, and the choice is wide. Consider your needs for the particular project. Will the garment be worn often? Will it be worn outdoors only, or will it do double duty against indoor chills as well? Should it be dressy? Elegance and warmth do quite well together in quilted clothing. Velvet, moiré, and satin look terrific and still have the practicality of warmth on their side when made into a snug quilted garment.

Being the practical sort, I most often choose wash-and-wear fabrics, things that require no special hand washing or dry cleaning, and with the exception of projects like the *Crazy Quilt Victorian Vest*, most of the projects in this book will reflect that practicality. Some purists insist on 100 percent cotton throughout, feeling that batting will beard, or work through polyester blends. Others say that polycottons pill after a while. But I think that if you choose a blend with a cotton content of at least 35 percent, you can avoid these problems.

Cottons and polycottons must *always* be washed and pressed before you cut, to allow for shrinkage or color fading. You will notice that polycottons will often be very soft after you wash them, and these soft pieces may be hard to piece together. The best way to overcome this problem is to starch the fabric before you cut it. Silks, satins, and velvets will be dry-cleaned; the only preparation for these fabrics is pressing (steaming for velvet) before you cut. And yes, wool is fine for quilting. Other napped fabrics such as corduroy should be washed like cotton fabrics but either pressed from the back or with the use of a needle board or Turkish towel. Be aware of direction of nap when cutting—but remember you *can* add interest by deliberately cutting against the nap direction. Avoid coating weight because the garment will end up very bulky; however, a wide range of lightweight wool is available. Wool should be steamed before it is cut.

A wide variety of prequilted fabrics are available to the home sewer. Several *Quiltwear* projects make good use of this option, and it is a shortcut to warmth and good looks I can recommend, with a few suggestions. When you are planning a garment for warmth and durability, as well as for good looks, choose a prequilted fabric with two "good" sides. That is, with a layer of fabric, then batting, then fabric again. This fabric is reversible and can form its own lining if you want. In the case of the *Rich Turkish Coat*, I used a prequilted fabric for the body of the garment but opted to line it separately for added warmth. It was a design decision as well—the fabric used on the reverse was undistinguished.

Be careful to buy a quilted fabric with a polyester batting; some intended for home-decorating use are filled with a kind of foam and do not drape or handle well.

Fairly lightweight prequilted reversibles were used in the robes seen in this book. Also available are thicker combinations intended for outerwear. These are double-sided as well, with an outing taffeta or poplinlike blend on one or both sides. This fabric, a poplin with a taffeta backing, was used for the man's *Warm, Padded Vest*.

Finally, look for the more formal prequilted fabrics. Velvets and satins, as well as soft loungewear knits, may be used for an elegant look.

The synthetic to avoid is rayon. Rayon does drape beautifully, and it often has a beautiful sheen. But its drapability makes it impossible to piece without ending up with hundreds of ripples. The final choice of fabric is, of course, yours. However, except when a very dressy look is intended, I recommend the polycottons.

Fabric is a forgiving medium, unlike wood or metal, which must be cut and joined exactly. As Hal Zina Bennett noted in his book, *Sewing for the Outdoors*, an eighth of an inch in cutting fabric is not all that critical one way or another. And unless you are trying to make a Mariner's Compass or a Grandmother's Flower Garden quilt, this is probably true. I encourage inventiveness—and enjoyment—in sewing. If something is mismeasured and does not fit for one reason or another, do not despair. Look for a way to enhance the mistake, a way to make it an area of interest. Quilted strips do not quite fit? Stitches showing? Cover the offending area with a band of contrasting bias tape or a bit of lace or trim. Remain open to design changes as you go along. In fact, incorporating "mistakes" into my final product is often what makes a design my own, and unique.

A wide variety of fabric prints and designs is available to the home sewer or designer. When I first began making patchwork projects twenty years ago, choices were extremely limited. It took a regular safari to find enough suitable prints. Today, patchwork is an art form, and stores everywhere cater to the designer with a dizzying array of calicoes and ginghams as well as a rainbow of solids.

1–1. Good value placement and print scale.

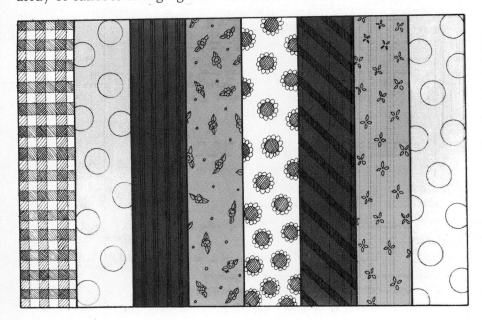

Try out your fabric combinations carefully before sewing them in place. Projects have a most pleasing look if one color dominates, a second has somewhat less importance, and a third provides accents in small areas. Use a variety of prints, keeping scale fairly consistent. Do not be afraid to experiment. If a larger-scale print furnishes you with just the right effect in a selection of small calicoes, use it! Quilted clothing is practical, yes—but it need not be boring. Design rules were made to be broken.

A final tip: choose tightly woven fabrics with an even weave unless you are prepared to fuse or back fabrics to prevent batting from "traveling." An even weave makes handling of more intricate shapes a much easier proposition as well.

Batting

Batting is what gives a quilt, whether it is a bed covering or a body covering, its "loft" or puffiness. The dead air space trapped between the backing and the outside layer is the true insulator, and the batting provides that space. A number of good batting choices can be made, but the word "batting" now generally refers to the polyester product so widely available. This is a good choice for the beginner, since it is easy to handle, evenly puffed, and strong. Be sure to buy a bonded batting. The bonding prevents bunching or pulling apart inside the garment and ensures that the batting will *remain* smooth, even after a number of washings.

Polyester batting is widely available in various widths, from 45 inches, for small projects, to bed-linen sizes. Thicknesses vary, too, from a very thin ¼-inch loft to the puffy batting generally used for comforters. The thinner batting is fine for lightweight clothing like the *Crazy Quilt Victorian Vest*, where warmth is not really the primary factor. The thicker battings provide more insulating value as they trap more of the body's heat.

Cotton batting, popular with generations of quilters, is less practical for quilted garments. It is thin and must be quilted very closely to prevent the batting from traveling when used or washed. The dense quality of the quilting cuts down on warmth since it brings the backing and top layer close together, trapping very little air. It also requires special care in handling and construction, as the cotton batting tears easily.

A possible alternative for lightweight garments is a layer of cotton flannel. This provides a bit of extra warmth and is easy to quilt. It is practical where small areas of trim on a garment are to be quilted, as on the *Seminole Shirt*. The collar, pocket flaps, cuffs, and yoke were fortified with a bit of flannel for warmth without excess puffiness.

More exotic batting materials are available if you feel adventurous. Silk batting is expensive, but it is pleasant to handle and warm. It requires care when cleaning the finished garment, of course, as does wool batting, which is also available in the United States and elsewhere. The insulating properties of wool have been known for centuries; wool batting was often used in the nineteenth century to add warmth to grandma's petticoats and grandpa's vests.

Batting Tips

- Be sure to choose the weight of batting needed for the project at hand.
- Silk and wool battings are very warm but are expensive and must be dry-cleaned (possibly hand-washed in cold water). Choose accordingly.
- Make sure batting is fully laid out (i.e., all folds pulled out flat) before cutting. Cut on a table or other hard surface, taking care not to stretch it as you cut, or it may contract to a size smaller than you need.
- Cut your garment piece or backing from fabric first, then use the fabric, rather than your paper pattern, as a guide to cut the batting.
- Pin batting in place carefully before cutting to ensure against crawling or slipping. If possible, pin all the way through batting.
- Cut ½ inch larger all around your fabric piece when using any but the lightest batting to allow for the natural loft of the filler. Fabric tends to move around a bit while machine sewing, and this will allow you some leeway. Excess batting can then be cut away from the fabric edges once the entire piece is quilted.

Sewing Machine

Elias Howe first patented his sewing machine in 1846, and home sewing has not been the same since. Quilting was once done entirely by hand, as was all sewing. Now you can choose whether you want the speed and convenience of machine quilting, the fine, slow craftsmanship of hand work, or a combination of the two. A quite effective look is to use hand quilting as an accent on a trim or yoke on a garment otherwise made by machine. As machine-sewn seams are usually stronger, this is a good idea for making a serviceable garment that will last for many years but still has the cachet of fine hand work.

A good sewing machine is a must, but by good, I do not necessarily mean fancy or expensive. The most dependable machine I ever owned was an ancient Singer that only sewed in a straight line—no zigzag, no blindstitch, and certainly no machine embroidery. It always made a good, strong seam, and I learned to work quite happily around its limitations. In fact, I still use some of the sewing techniques I was forced to learn because of the simplicity of my machine; and I will include them in this book.

Your sewing machine is your greatest ally, but it does require care. Oil it often—after every project, at least—and *use* that little brush that came with your machine. A buildup of lint under the feed dog and around the bobbin can form a thick, feltlike mass that can throw off the alignment of your entire machine. If your thread breaks often, change your needle. A slightly bent needle may not show to the naked eye, but it can be enough to snap your thread time after frustrating time. The same goes for tiny nicks caused by sewing over pins. A #14 needle is most often used, but a heavier one may be just what you need for heavier fabrics or thick batting. Try a #16 if the lighter needle seems reluctant or continues to break often.

Important Supplies

You will probably have many of these supplies already on hand if you do any sewing at all. Others will prove handy for your quilting projects and should become a part of your sewing staples.

- □ *Thread*   The most commonly available thread today is cotton-wrapped polyester. It is strong and comes in a wide variety of colors and weights. Heavy fabrics may require a heavier thread; ask when you buy your fabric. Silk or 100 percent cotton thread is also available, but cotton thread sometimes shrinks in washing, causing seams to pucker.
- □ *Good fabric scissors*   These are needed for cutting fabric quickly and accurately.
- □ *Paper scissors*   An old pair is useful for cutting paper patterns and plastic or sandpaper templates for patchwork shapes.
- □ *Tailor's chalk, pencil, or water-soluble "invisible" felt-tip marker*   Use these to mark templates and fabric shapes.
- □ *Clear plastic ruler*   You will need a ruler at least 18 inches long and 2 inches wide for marking and measuring fabric strips. These may be purchased in fabric stores but may be less expensive in art or office-supply stores.
- □ *Measuring tape*   A tape is invaluable for taking your own (or someone else's) measurements.
- □ *Plastic T-square*   This is handy for making sure fabric is squared and true.
- □ *Straight pins*   Ball-point, dressmaker's, and T pins are useful.
- □ *Pincushion*   This keeps your pins handy. If your pincushion comes with an emery bag, use it to keep pins and needles sharp.
- □ *Needles*   You will need sewing machine needles (#14 and #16), hand sewing needles, and quilting needles.
- □ *Graph paper*   Use this to plan out designs and patterns. Four squares to the inch is about right.
- □ *Sandpaper*   Medium grit is great for templates; put grit-side down on fabric for a nonslip grip.
- □ *Heavy plastic*   Buy this by the sheet or save large coffee can lids and use for templates.
- □ *Mat board or cardboard*   Custom-width strips are a boon when you use the string quilting technique. Cut whatever width you want, from 2 inches to 6 or 7 inches wide and at least 18 inches long. Use the templates to mark lines on fabric or to guide a circular fabric cutting wheel.
- □ *Utility knife*   You will need this for cutting templates from your mat board or plastic.
- □ *Glue stick*   This tool can be used to hold pattern pieces together or to hold fabrics for appliqué.
- □ *Bias tape*   Bias tape can be used to cover raw edges, as a design element, or to bind seams.
- □ *Closures*   Velcro, snaps, buttons, "frogs," and ties should all be standard equipment in your sewing box.
- □ *Embroidery floss*   Fancy stitchery is a wonderful accent.
- □ *Laces, trims, ribbons*   Use for creative, feminine touches. You should save all scraps for crazy quilting.

These tools are not necessities, but they will make your quilting more enjoyable *and* more professional.

- □ *Quilting frame*   You will need a frame or large hoop for projects you may want to embellish—or accomplish!—with hand quilting unless you are that rare quilter who prefers to work without.
- □ *Embroidery hoop*   This is invaluable for fancy stitchery. If the hoop is large enough it could double as a quilting frame. Many hoops are available with stands; this leaves both hands free for stitching.
- □ *Rotary cutter*   This is a relatively new tool that looks something like a pizza cutter. It is used with a heavy plastic cutting board to protect both the razor-sharp blade and your tabletop. It makes short work of cutting uniform strips when used with a mat board template.

Design

The ideas in this book are intended to get you started. Go as far as your imagination dictates and your pocketbook allows.

In planning your own designs, graph paper is a big help. Using one square as one inch, you can map out a design as simple or as elaborate as you might wish. Colored pencils are often used to help plan color placement and design for patchwork squares as well as for entire garments. Graph paper can be used to plan cutting diagrams for your own "designer clothes" as well.

When using graph paper designs, convert squares to inches on your fabric and be sure to add the necessary seam allowances. One-fourth inch is usually sufficient for patchwork areas, but stress-bearing garment seams should be at least ½ inch.

Quilt designs can be adapted to your use. Books are a fine source of inspiration, as are magazines and some newspapers. See the *Sourcebooks* section of this book for some fine resources to help inspire you.

Designs—and inspiration—are everywhere. Baskets provide fascinating patterns that could become design elements. Nature is full of design ideas. Look around on a nice long walk: brick walls, for example, provide interesting sources of patchwork patterns. Or look to other forms of needlework. I have used graphed needlepoint designs to plan out Seminole patchwork. If the design is simple, with a number of repeats, the conversion works very well. Knitting and crochet designs could have the same versatility.

In many cases, a simple rough sketch on regular paper is sufficient. Some of the ideas in this book never made it "down in black and white" at all. For the *Doggie Coat*, for instance, I simply knew I planned a Log Cabin variation called Courthouse Steps. It would be slightly out of square since the coat is longer than it is wide. Log Cabin variations are so simple that it was only necessary to know the overall size of the coat (which depends on the dog). Then I could plan the width of the strips and begin.

Patterns

Since people come in all sizes and shapes, patterns per se will not be included here. I will, however, show you how to adapt a commercial pattern so you have a perfectly fitted, personalized, practical, and warm garment.

Specific pattern numbers are also not included; pattern manufacturers change their designs so often that any such numbers would be obsolete by the time you read this. The exception is the Folkwear, Inc., line. These numbers *do* stay the same.

Choose a simple design, one with few darts or extra seams, when you buy a pattern. Princess seams are not particularly suited to the extra bulk of quilted clothing, so try to avoid patterns that use them. Sleeves can be a problem in a padded garment. In very bulky designs, a set-in sleeve can prove difficult. If you are a beginner you may want to stick with an oriental-style dropped or kimono sleeve, or a raglan style. Try looking in the "easy" or "learn to sew" sections of the pattern book first. Until you are used to looking for simple, adaptable designs elsewhere in the book, you may find what you need there. When you have made a few things, even designer patterns become fair game.

While it is not necessary to choose a pattern intended for quilting, you may wish to do so, especially at first. The directions are clear and concise and usually include many worthwhile hints on quilting that you can incorporate into later projects.

In using a pattern not intended for quilting, I often buy one size larger to allow for the added thickness of the finished garment. This is not necessary if you are using cotton flannel as a batting material, or even the thin polyester batt, but the thicker batts seem to work better if you allow yourself room to move about in the clothes. If you plan to use a pattern you have on hand, simply add ½ inch to the side seams.

Make any necessary changes in the pattern tissue itself. There are lines printed on the tissue to guide you. If the pattern is too long, fold along the line and pin or tape in place. If it is too short, cut along the line, add a piece of tissue or paper of the necessary width, and pin or tape in place. A longer vest can become a bolero in this way, or a jacket can become a coat.

Use your imagination! If you find a pattern that fits and works well for you, use it over and over and change it for various projects from long to short and back again. Add sleeves to make a vest into a jacket or coat, or leave sleeves off to make a vest. Necklines can be varied easily—cut a rounded neck into a **V** or **U** shape, and point or round the bottom as desired (fig. 1–2). A pattern is just a place to start —*you* are the designer.

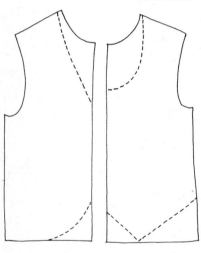

1–2. Change your paper pattern as needed.

Color

Artists and designers traditionally have used a device called a color wheel to help them plan and visualize a color scheme.

Red, yellow, and blue are the primary colors. They are pure and unmixed hues. The secondary colors occur when any two of the primary colors are mixed: red and blue make purple, red and yellow make orange, and yellow and blue make green. These colors are placed between the primaries on the arbitrary circle of the color wheel. Green is opposite red, orange is opposite blue, and purple is opposite yellow. These relationships of secondary to primary colors are called complementary; the colors go well together, or complement each other, and seem to set up a kind of vibration. You will probably recognize the holiday combo of red and green, but the others are serviceable as well.

Now, by mixing a primary and the nearest adjacent secondary color, we have tertiary colors—red and orange make red-orange, yellow and green make yellow-green, and so on. Artists often use three colors occurring side by side in the wheel, creating a harmonious if safe choice. More exciting, perhaps, are color schemes using any three colors of equal distances on the wheel. The primaries themselves make a delightful child's crayon-box scheme, but more subtle choices would be maroon (red-purple), teal (blue-green), and yellow-orange.

Warm family colors—the reds through yellows—or the cool family—purples through greens—make harmonious color schemes for the designer.

Tints—the pastel colors—or grayed, subtle hues of the pure colors allow a wide range of choice.

Experiment with color swatches, or perhaps make up a sampler pillow top to get the feel of how your colors work together before launching a major project. A quick way to get an idea of how colors will look together is to cut, to scale, sample squares of the fabrics you might want to use. With glue stick, attach them to a piece of cardboard to create a "fabric graph." Because glue stick dries slowly, you can lift the squares and rearrange the colors to get an idea of how they will look in different combinations.

Cutting

Fancy shapes and fabric strips need to be uniform for best results, but cutting can become tedious unless you know a few quick tricks. Here is where your clear plastic ruler comes in handy. The markings are visible along the width of the ruler as well as the length, so you can see through to the line marked on your fabric for the previous strip. Any width up to 2 inches can easily be seen and as quickly marked. Fabric shops sell special quilting rulers that can be quite expensive, but office supply and artists' supply stores also carry clear rulers in various widths from 1 to 3 inches that may be cheaper.

For fabric strips used in string quilting, lay the ruler directly on the fabric and mark using a lead pencil, "invisible" (water-soluble) felt-tip, or tailor's chalk. Several layers may be cut at once if it is not necessary to follow a repeat print or plaid. Cut along your lines using sharp scissors or a rotary cutter and a protective plastic shield. If you want wider strips, cut a template from mat board, cardboard, or plastic and proceed as usual.

Patchwork shapes can be cut uniformly by making a template from cardboard, sandpaper, or heavy plastic. Draw around the template. This line becomes your stitching line, so always mark on the back side of the fabric. Allow ¼ inch for seam allowance and cut along that line. This works well for geometrics as well as curved shapes.

Fabric stores carry ¼-inch square rods used to mark seam allowances on straight-edged pieces. Also available are special holders for two pencils in tandem, held approximately ¼ inch apart. One pencil marks the stitching line, the other automatically marks the cutting line. Care must be taken on curves, but unless you have a good eye for freehand cutting, this trick is a boon. Incidentally, the same effect can be obtained by binding two pencils together with strong rubber bands at top and bottom—just make sure the points are even with each other.

String Quilting Basics

Many of the designs in this book are worked with the string quilting technique. This is based on an old technique used for years by thrifty quiltmakers. These quiltmakers solved the problem of what to do with long scraps too narrow to piece together. They simply stitched them to a muslin backing. What started out as a random effort soon turned into a science, and such string patterns as the Spider Web and the Mountain Star were developed. Often the strips were sewn onto a backing cut in a specific shape, a tulip or a triangle, for example.

The string quilting technique in this book is based on these ideas. But it goes further. The backing "shape" is a pattern piece, and the patchwork top, batting, and backing are sewn in the sewing machine at the same time for a strong, handsome, machine-quilted finish. Jean Wells string quilts directly onto the batting alone, and adds lining separately for a more finished and more conventional "lining" look. There are a few basics that will make your projects easy as well as beautiful and professional-looking.

- Cut batting 1½ inches larger than the backing piece all around to allow for shifting and the natural "loft" of the batt.
- Position batting over backing and let the excess lap over on all sides. Use tailor tacks (see *Sewing Tips*) rather than pins to hold batting in position; you avoid trapping pins inside the garment—a painful proposition—or breaking a sewing machine needle on pins hidden between the layers. An alternative method is to pin only the edges (with color ball or T pins) and remove pins as you sew. This is more acceptable for small projects than for a large one like a jacket or coat, since the batting may tend to shift from the weight of a bigger project.
- To make sure your design is even—and comes out that way in the end—always start quilting at the *middle* of the back, or at the *front edge* of a jacket or vest. Measure carefully to find the middle.
- Sew your middle piece in place along both edges, then sew on each succeeding strip. Press strips away from the middle and add another strip until you reach the edges.
- The inside of your string quilted garment will be beautifully finished and will need no lining. However, if you want extra warmth, use muslin as your backing fabric and use your tissue pattern to cut a lining from different fabric. Remember to make any adjustments to the lining that you made to the garment.

This patchwork technique was developed by the Seminole Indians early in the twentieth century. It is similar to string quilting because you will sew long strips of fabric together. But these strips are then carefully measured and cut. The new pieces are then rearranged and sewn together.

Seminole patchwork is much easier to do than it looks. It is traditionally done by machine; but it needs all the accuracy you can muster, and it does require patience. A clear plastic ruler is a must, and a rotary cutter is a very big help.

□ Cottons and polycottons are best for Seminole work. Because of the size of the strips and the frequent cutting and handling, this work requires fabric that does not ravel easily and takes pressing well.

□ Starch the fabric before you cut. This helps to stabilize the long, narrow strips, which do tend to stretch.

□ If your presser foot measures ¼ inch from the needle, use it as your seam guide. If not, mark a ¼-inch guide with masking tape on the soleplate of your sewing machine.

□ A rotary cutter is best for cutting because the fabric always stays flat on the cutting surface. This reduces the chances of wavy cutting lines. If you do not own a rotary cutter, mark the lines with tailor's chalk or a pencil and cut *carefully* with very sharp scissors.

□ You may end up with inaccurate, wavy lines if you sew narrow strips with the fabric always to the left of the needle and the seam allowance always to the right. Try this method. Sew the first seam in the normal way. Then sew the second seam using the first line of stitches as a sewing guide instead of the cut edges (fig. 1–3). Keep the *left* edge of your presser foot lined up with the previous row of stitches to produce a uniform line.

□ Take care not to stretch your piecework when pressing.

For many *Quiltwear* projects, a quilting frame is not a necessity. If you wish, try a 15- to 18-inch oval or circular hoop.

Special needles and waxed quilting threads are best for hand quilting. Use a single 18-inch strand of thread and knot the end you cut from the spool. This will help prevent tangling as you quilt. Pull the knot through the backing fabric as shown in figure 1–3 to "lose" the knot. Make small running stitches ¹⁄₁₆ inch from the edge of the piece; stitch "in the ditch" (or seam) when you do not want the stitches to be noticeable. Experienced quilters can make a number of even, tiny stitches at a time, but two or three stitches running are easier to pull through the fabric and batting. A thimble is a help here if you can use one.

Lose the knot again at the end of your line of stitching by making a small single knot close to the surface of the fabric on the back side. Pull backing and front fabric apart at that point and the knot should pop through to the batting.

You can get as creative as you like with quilting. Try diamond or feather designs on larger areas. Many of the projects in this book

Seminole Work Basics

1–3. Use your previous stitching line as a sewing guide.

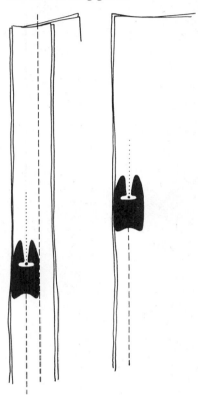

Hand Quilting Tips

have been chosen to keep the stitching rather simple and maintain the insulating value of the loft wherever possible.

Sewing Tips

Here are a few basic tips to make your finished garments fit better, look better, and last longer.

- □ Most patterns allow ⅝ inch for seam allowances. For quilted garments I often use a ½-inch seam to allow a bit extra for the batting, particularly if I have not bought a larger-than-normal pattern.
- □ The best all-around setting for the machine seems to be twelve stitches to the inch. Heavier fabrics may need fewer stitches to the inch, but no fewer than eight or seams will be more basted than sewn and will not stand the stress of wear. A heavier thread is needed for strength if fewer than twelve stitches are used.
- □ Backstitch three or four stitches at the ends of your seams to prevent pulling loose.
- □ Tailor tacks are used to hold batting, backing, and top layers together, or to hold batting and backing in place. Using heavy thread in a contrasting color, take one stitch through all layers. Cut ends, leaving at least 1-inch tag ends on the wrong side of fabric. Make tacks 2 to 3 inches apart, as needed. You may tie the ends—you should if the garment will get a great deal of handling during the construction—but it is usually unnecessary. Of course, it is much easier to remove the tacks when the job is completed if they are not tied, since you only need grasp one loose end and pull out the stitch.
- □ Topstitching may be used to complete a garment, to add contrasting trim, to strengthen a seam, or to finish bias trimming. Most sewing machines have gauges beside the feed dog to help keep topstitching (and seam allowances) uniform, but I often use the outer edge of the presser foot as a guide, especially when topstitching an open seam when the gauge is hidden by fabric. Even speed and a steady hand are all that is really needed, but some people like to mark their topstitching lines with tailor's chalk.

Seam Finishes

The inside of a garment is almost as important as the outside—and can be as beautiful. Some of my quilted clothes are almost reversible, since I like the effect of contrasting bias binding, which becomes a design element in the finished product. There are a number of choices, though, that you may wish to explore. There are increasing degrees of difficulty, so you may want to use the easier finishes for simpler projects, and the nicer finishes for more elegant garments.

Lining is a second alternative that nearly does away with the need for seam finishes, and it will be dealt with in the appropriate chapters.

- □ The easiest of the seam finishes is a pinked edge, which is a zigzag or scalloped edge made by special pinking or scalloping shears.

□ Zigzagging the raw edges is a more effective method to prevent raveling—fast and easy, but hardly beautiful. Your sewing machine can make quick work of this. It works best to zigzag garment pieces before joining them, but this can be done afterward.

□ Bias bindings in matching or contrasting colors are an elegant finish. They may be used on inner seams to give a designer look or on outside edges where lining does not eliminate the raveling.

Commercial bias tape comes in many colors, and even calico prints. It is available in double fold (¼-inch wide), single fold (½-inch wide), and wide (1 inch). Hem facing and blanket binding are other choices. Wide bias tape is most useful for finishing projects for adults, but the double fold can be used on children's clothing if the batting is not too thick. It also works well on garments where an understated effect is wanted, but again, it must be used in conjunction with a thin batting. Hem facing can be used as it is intended, turned under and hidden, or to make a strong design statement as a wide band of color.

Bias tape is actually easy to work with. Open the bias tape and stitch along the edge in the folded line, as shown (fig. 1–4). Fold to the inside and stitch by hand (fig. 1–5). If I plan a machine finish, as on a more casual garment, I sew first on the inside, turn to the outside, and edgestitch carefully close to the edge of the bias tape.

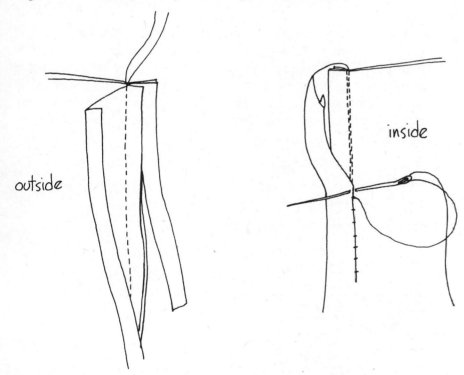

1–4. Sew bias tape in place.   **1–5.** Finish by hand.

The new tricot bindings are used in much the same way to prevent raveling of single inside seams. Enclose both raw edges of the fabric by lapping with binding and then edgestitching.

You may wish to use a matching bias edging cut from one of your own fabrics. This is a relatively simple operation, and the effect is well worth the extra effort. Start by cutting two 9-inch squares of fabric, using your T-square or a triangle to be sure the square is true. Cut from point A to point B on the bias, as shown in figure 1–6. Sew

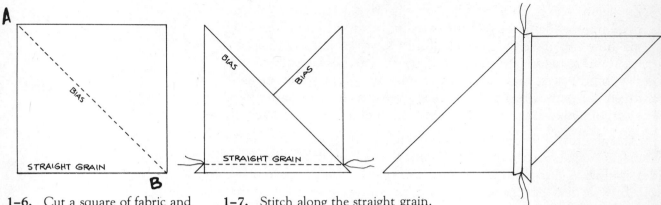

1–6. Cut a square of fabric and find the true bias.

1–7. Stitch along the straight grain.

the triangles together, along the straight grain of the fabric (fig. 1–7). Press seam open. Then sew pieces together to form a bias strip. Mark 1½-inch lines as shown in figure 1–8.

Sew bias strip together as shown, using a ¼-inch seam. Cut along the drawn lines to form a continuous bias strip (fig. 1–9).

To use your homemade bias tape, fold it lengthwise so the edges are together, keeping the seam allowances inside. Press. Sew in place as shown, with raw edge along the edge of your garment. Fold over and hand stitch along pressed edge, or simply edgestitch by machine.

□ A flat-felled seam is particularly useful on quilted clothes that will not be lined and that will receive a lot of wear or frequent washings. Sew your seam as usual, ⅝ inch wide. Trim one seam allowance to a scant ¼ inch and press both seam allowances to one side. Fold under the wider seam allowance so it covers the narrow seam allowance. Edgestitch along the fold so it encloses the seam.

1–8. Sew together.

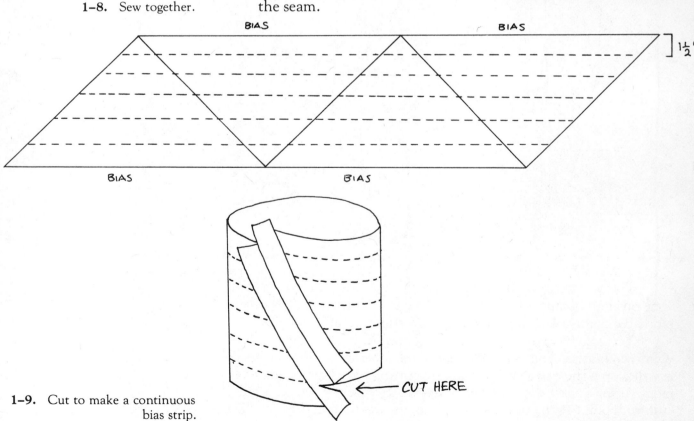

1–9. Cut to make a continuous bias strip.

DOGGIE COAT

Our pets' fur coats probably keep them warm enough in the house—even with drastically lowered thermostats—but it is a kindness to provide them with a little help on subzero days for that morning constitutional.

The *Doggie Coat* is an easy project and a good way to learn all the basics of string quilting. It appears first in this book because it is a beginner's project and will help you learn terms and techniques (and because I am fond of animals). If you have no dog (or cat) or do not want to start with this project, just look it over. It will help you with some of the other projects.

I chose the popular Courthouse Steps quilt pattern for this coat. It is both simple and effective. Purchase a commercial dog coat pattern. Several are available from the major pattern companies. I have altered one for this project, since the one I bought was unnecessarily complicated.

Yardages will vary somewhat depending on the size of your dog—a coat for a Yorkie will be much smaller than a coat for an Irish wolfhound. The following yardages will give you an idea of what you will need for an average-sized animal. Remember that the coat will receive hard outdoor wear, so the fabric should be washable. A cotton blend would be fine, but corduroy and washable wool are also good choices.

Materials

- ☐ dog coat pattern
- ☐ ½ yard of solid fabric (for backing)
- ☐ ¼ yard *each* of three different fabrics—plaids, prints, or solids
- ☐ ½ yard of bonded quilt batting
- ☐ one package of wide bias tape in a contrasting color
- ☐ one 3-inch strip of Velcro strip fasteners
- ☐ one package of Velcro dot fasteners
- ☐ one spool of thread to match color of backing

Directions

1. Measure your dog from his neck to just above his tail and from side to side. Adjust the pattern as necessary to make sure the coat will come down well over his sides for warmth (see directions in *Beginnings*).
2. Lay out your pattern on the backing. Pin and cut. Cut a 4-inch square from a solid color.
3. Cut polyester quilt batting (using the same pattern). You may wish to allow ¼ inch on all sides to allow for the thickness of the batting. The excess will be trimmed away later.
4. Use tailor tacks to attach batting as shown in *Beginnings*. Pins may be used on a small project such as this if you are careful to place them only on the edges and to remove them all as you work.
5. Position the 4-inch square exactly in the center of the back as measured from side to side (fig. 2–1). It may be placed a bit forward of the center on the lengthwise dimension. Pin.
6. Cut two matching 2-inch-by-4-inch strips in a contrasting fabric.

Lay them face down along the horizontal edges of the center patch as shown in figure 2–2. Stitch through all layers.

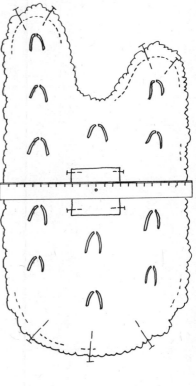

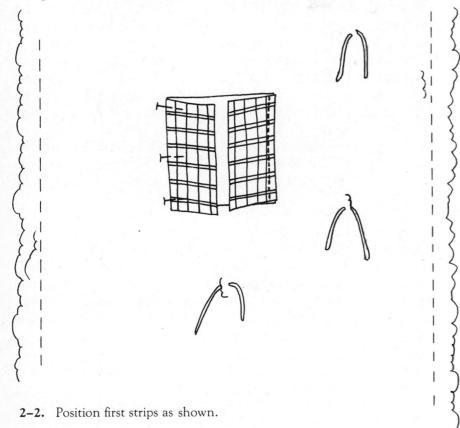

2–2. Position first strips as shown.

7. Turn strips back and press away from the center (fig. 2–3).

2–3. Lap next strips and turn back.

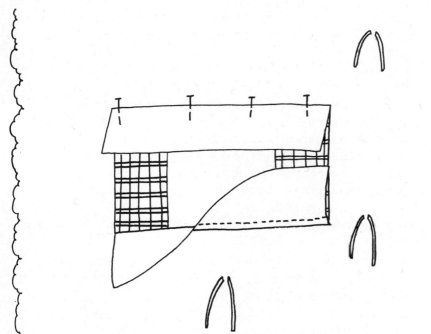

2–4. See step 10.

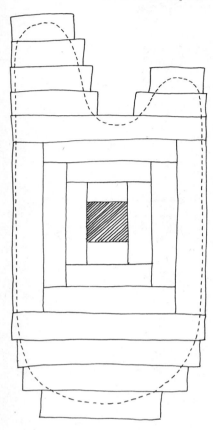

2–5. Sew undercarriage in place.

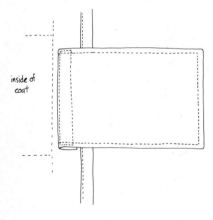

inside of coat

8. Measure two strips 2 inches wide by the length of the center square plus the two strips already sewn down. Lay these along the lengthwise edge of these two pieces of fabric, covering the raw edges and pin. Stitch through all layers, fold back, and press.

9. Continue to add on 2-inch-wide strips until you reach the edge of your backing; use progressively longer strips of fabric to cover the raw edges of fabric on alternate sides of your original square.

10. When you complete the Courthouse Steps square, you will be left with areas around the neck and tail that will need quilting. Keep adding strips until you come to the ends of the coat. Do not worry about the square edges hanging over; they will be trimmed away. This method does away with the need for precisely shaped pieces to follow the curve of the edge and wastes very little fabric (fig. 2–4).

11. Press the coat from the top.

12. Using the backing as a guide, cut away excess fabric and batting. Edgestitch around the coat to hold all layers together.

13. Bind the edges with contrasting bias tape. Work in a bit of "ease" around the curves by pushing a little surplus bias tape under the presser foot with the eraser end of a pencil as you sew. This will make enough extra fabric to fit around the curves when you turn the bias tape to cover raw edges.

14. Stitch tape in place.

15. To make undercarriage closure, cut four pieces of fabric, each 4 inches by 6 inches. (If your dog is stout you may need to extend these pieces to the necessary length. Be sure to measure from the side edges of the coat under his belly before cutting, and make the pieces long enough to overlap by at least 1½ inches.) Cut two pieces of batting the same size.

16. Pin two fabric pieces together with right sides together. Position batting on top, pin, and stitch through all layers on three sides, ½ inch from the edge. Leave one end free. (Tip: If you find it difficult to sew directly over batting, place tissue paper on top of the batting and sew through that. Tear away paper after the pieces are sewn together.) Repeat for other two fabric pieces.

17. Clip excess fabric at corners, then turn right side out. Press.

18. Topstitch ¼ inch from the edges for a finished look.

19. Turn under the raw edge of each flap. Pin on the underside of the coat and stitch in place as shown in figure 2–5. They should be positioned just behind the dog's front legs, allowing him room for free movement. Try the coat on your pet to find correct placement and pin the flaps in place. A zigzag stitch may be used here.

20. Sew two Velcro pieces to these extensions for an adjustable closure.

21. If your dog is barrel-chested, add an extension to the chest-collar piece in the same manner; add only a left-hand flap.

22. To finish the chest pieces, fit the coat on your dog and pin. Mark, then sew Velcro dots in place for a snug fit. You may prefer a button and buttonhole on the chest for a more finished effect, but Velcro works best on the "undercarriage" (fig. 2–6). It will allow for growth or weight loss and will make removal of a wet or muddy coat much easier.

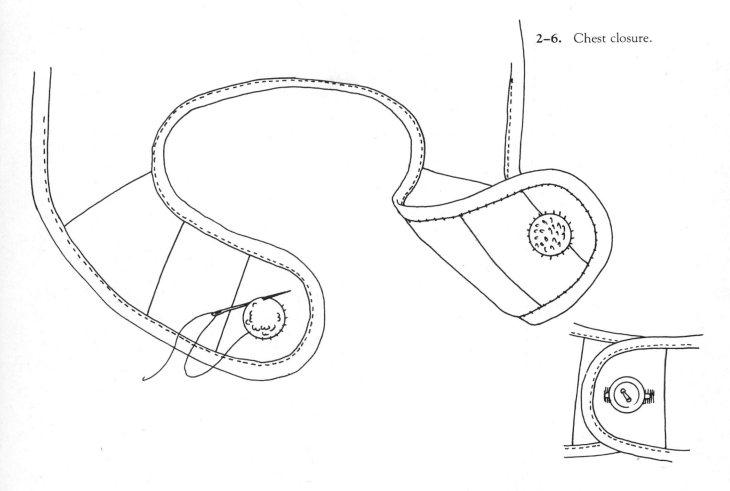

Experiment with color and fabric placement to create interest. Try one of the examples shown or design your own (fig. 2–7).

If you would like to try something extra, appliqué a bone or a ball in the central square, or personalize it with your dog's name in embroidery stitches.

You can easily piece this project in the Log Cabin pattern. See the *Woman's Side-closing Double-padded Vest.*

The Personal Touch

2–7. Two piecing variations.

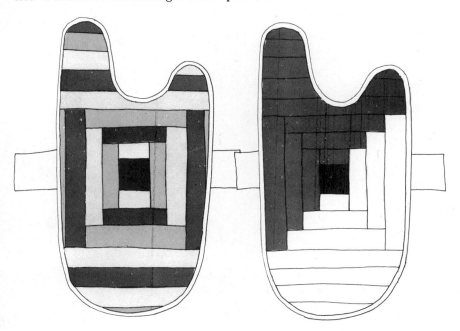

MAN'S SIMPLE INDOOR/OUTDOOR VEST

CATHY JOHNSON

This vest is another easy project for the beginner. It is also toasty warm. My husband wore his vest all through the coldest winter on record in our area, and he was often so warm that he would have to take his coat off.

Any uncomplicated vest pattern from one of the major pattern companies can form the basis for the vest. Just look for a pattern without darts or excess detail; avoid welted pockets and fitted silk backs. Since the vest will be quilted, any extra detailing would make this final product too bulky. The pattern I chose offered two views, either of which would have been a good choice for a quilted vest. If you already have a vest pattern that you like, keep in mind that you can eliminate such details as pockets or belts to simplify the project.

The materials you need will of course depend on the pattern and size that you choose. A cotton or polyester would be a good fabric choice, but you could use a lightweight wool or corduroy for extra warmth. The vest I made (see the color section for a photograph) called for the following amounts.

Materials

- vest pattern
- 2 ¼ yards of solid fabric
- ½ yard of plaid fabric for trim
- 1 ½ yards of bonded quilt batting (I like to use a thicker batting for winter wear, but you may want lightweight simply to add a puffy-quilted effect)
- two packages of wide bias tape in a matching color
- six decorative gripper-snap closures
- one spool of thread to match solid fabric

Directions

1. Simplify your pattern by lapping any unnecessary seams. My pattern had two side seams, one just in front of the underarm and one a few inches to the back. I eliminated the seam to the back, opting to keep the one closest to a normal underarm seam. To do this, lap the seam, pinning pattern pieces together at the seam line and proceed as usual to lay out your pattern.
2. Cut backing from the solid fabric. You could use something more daring, if you like. (I once lined a vest for my husband using an all-over small-print beagle pattern—a good choice for a dog lover!) Follow your adjusted pattern, remembering any changes you made to simplify the project. Allow an extra ½ inch at the side seams to allow for the padding effect of the batting.
3. Use your backing piece as a pattern to cut batting, allowing an extra ½ inch on all sides for quilting ease. (The excess will be trimmed away later.)
4. See *Beginnings* for hints on cutting strips. From the solid fabric, cut as many 4-inch strips as possible. Do not worry at this point about length of the strips; selvage-to-selvage width is fine. Do cut strips from the scrap pieces left after you cut the backing—just be careful not to cut on the bias. These short strips can be used in smaller areas.

5. Cut one 4-inch square from the plaid fabric for the center back patch. Then cut as many 2-inch strips from the plaid as you can.

6. Use tailor tacks to secure batting to backing.

7. Review the section on string quilting in *Beginnings*. Pin center trim piece in the middle of the back, directly on top of the batting. Be sure to measure from side to side to find the center. It is all right for the piece to be a bit below vertical center, but it must be exactly centered from each side or your 4-inch strips will not come out even as you reach the sides of the vest.

8. Cut two 4-inch pieces from one of your solid strips (forming 4-inch squares). Pin as shown in figure 3–1 to the sides of the center back patch, then sew through all layers (trim, batting, patch, and backing fabric), taking a ¼-inch seam. Press seams flat. You will have three squares in a row, with seams between them holding them firmly to the batting and backing.

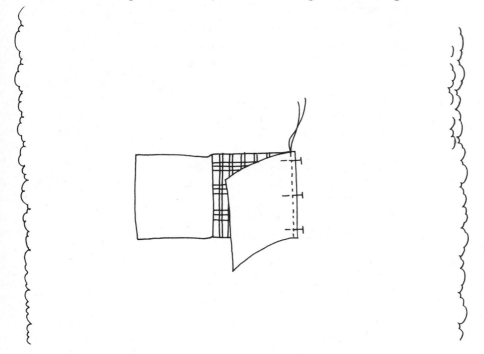

3–1. Add a solid square to each side of your central square.

9. Position a 4-inch-wide solid rectangle over the top of all three squares to find the proper length. Cut two. Pin these squares to the top and bottom of the row of squares and stitch, still taking a ¼-inch seam (fig. 3–2). Press these two pieces away from the center squares.

10. Continue piecing rectangles over the ends of each set of strips, alternating between sides and top and bottom until you reach the side seams. This will form a square on the back of your vest. Do not worry if some of the fabric hangs over the edges of the backing piece. This will be trimmed.

11. You will notice that you have uncovered batting at the top and bottom of your square. Continue adding strips until you come to the edge of the vest backing. Define the yoke at the top of the vest back with a 2-inch strip of plaid fabric.

3–2. Lap rectangles over squares.

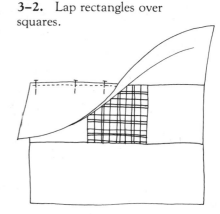

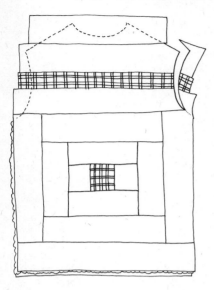

3-3. Cut away excess.

3-4. Add plaid strip to cover raw edges.

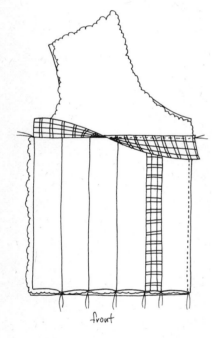

front

3-5. Finish shoulders.

12. Use the backing piece as a guide to trim away excess through all layers where strips overlap cutting lines (fig. 3-3).

13. Decide how high you want your yoke detail in front, and cut enough 4-inch strips to go from the center front to the side seams, measuring from the vest bottom to the yoke. Cut two 2-inch pieces of plaid fabric this same length.

14. Begin sewing strips at the center front edge of the vest, catching the first strip firmly at the edge. Add strips as shown until you come to the side seam. Include your 2-inch plaid strips for trim, or omit them if you want a simpler effect.

15. Sew a 2-inch plaid strip across the yoke line, making sure to cover the upper edges of your vertical strips neatly and hide any raw edges (fig. 3-4). Continue piecing to the top edges of the shoulder line. Here is your chance to use some of those shorter strips.

16. To make a finished-looking shoulder, use one of the 2-inch plaid strips. Use the backing piece as a cutting guide and cut away excess batting and body fabric at the shoulder line so you can see the slope of the shoulder. Lay a 2-inch strip parallel to the shoulder line, 1½ inches away from the line. Sew along the edge of the strip closest to the shoulder and fold it up to lie flat in a line with the shoulder (fig. 3-5). Press well.

17. With right sides together, take ⅝-inch seams at the sides and shoulders.

18. Sew wide bias tape along these seams; trim seam allowance and batting to ¼ inch. Turn bias tape to cover all raw edges and stitch down by hand.

19. Trim all remaining edges (armholes, neckline, bottom of vest, etc.) even with the backing piece and bind with bias tape as you did the inner seams, hand finishing on the inside. Add gripper snaps according to the manufacturer's directions.

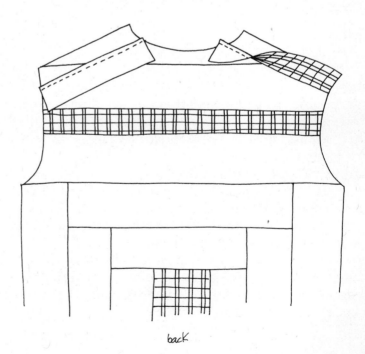

back

Try different fabric combinations. A lightweight denim could work here for the top layer, with a Glen plaid backing and trim. Dark brown also looks good with a rich plaid trim. Experiment for a personal look.

You might prefer a slanted yoke in front (fig. 3–6). Try it for a different effect, perhaps varying the shape of the bottom as well.

3–6. A yoke variation.

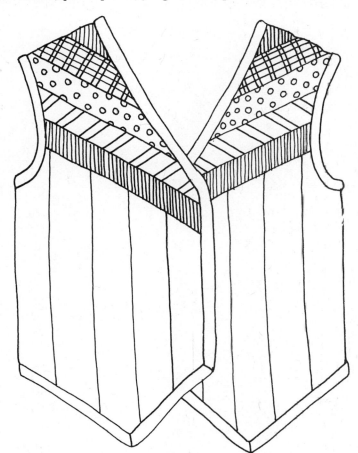

WOMAN'S SIDE-CLOSING DOUBLE-PADDED VEST

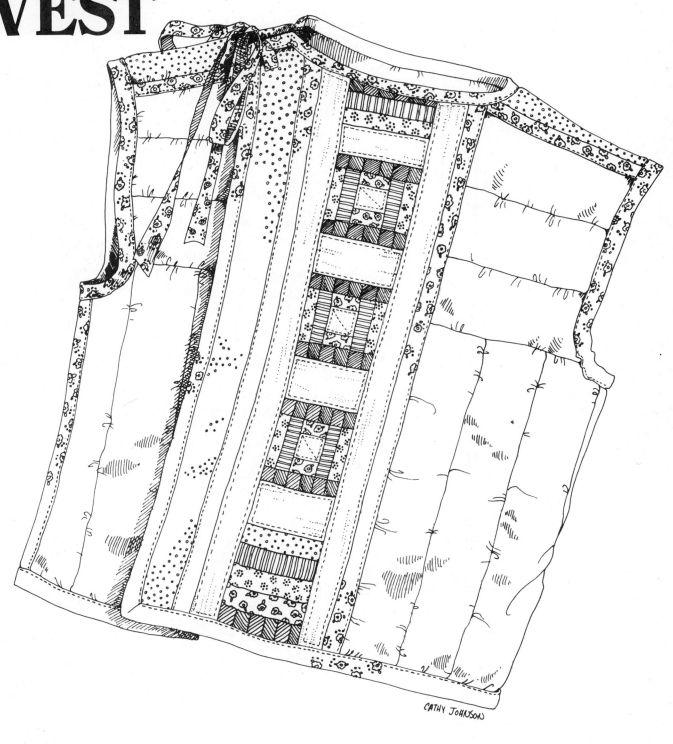

CATHY JOHNSON

The double (or extra-thick) padding and front-wrapped design that provides an additional layer across the front make this an especially warm vest. It goes well with a solid-colored turtleneck sweater and straight-legged jeans or slacks.

When I made this vest there were no vest or jacket patterns with asymmetrical closings available. A Vogue blouse pattern worked well, however, demonstrating that it *is* possible to adapt almost any pattern to your needs; I just left off the sleeves and shortened the blouse tails. At this writing, at least one of the major pattern companies (Butterick) carries a similar pattern intended to be used as a vest or jacket. If you cannot find a pattern, however, do not be afraid to experiment with what is available. This is one way to make your clothing really individual.

This vest combines hand and machine quilting, and so requires a bit more time than the first two projects. The construction and the extra batting make this a project for lightweight fabrics only. The heavier fabrics will lead to a very bulky vest, so stick with the polycottons. As usual, yardages depend on the size of the pattern used. The yardages given here (for the vest shown in the color section) are for sizes 10–12.

Materials

- □ vest pattern
- □ fabric A: 2¾ yards of solid fabric (for body and backing)
- □ fabric B: ¼ yard of light fabric (for center panel)
- □ fabric C: 1½ yard of dark print fabric (for bias binding and quilted trim)
- □ fabric D: ¼ yard of fabric—choose a contrasting color (for block centers and back trim)
- □ quilt-block fabric: ¼ yard each of four different fabrics—plaids, solids, or prints
- □ 1½ yards of extra-thick bonded quilt batting *or* 2 yards of lightweight batting
- □ one spool of thread to match color of fabric A
- □ one spool of quilting thread to match color of fabric A
- □ one package of Velcro dot fasteners
- □ one package of wide bias tape for inside seams

Directions

1. Make any changes or adjustments on your pattern. If you are using a pattern intended for another use (such as my blouse pattern), try pinning pattern pieces together to check the fit. You may want to make a muslin dummy of the main pattern pieces. Pin pattern to fabric A and add ½ inch extra at side seams and armhole tops, as you will be using extra padding. Cut.
2. See section on batting in *Beginnings*. Pin backing to batting, allowing an extra ½ inch, and cut batting. Hold batting in place on backing pieces with tailor tacks. (Since the batting is thicker than normal it is best not to take the chance of losing pins in the extra loft. Color ball or T pins may be used with care around the edges.)

3. Plan out front design on paper. You will have room for three 3½-inch squares and string quilted trim top and bottom or four 3½-inch squares without the additional trim. I used the Courthouse Steps variation of the Log Cabin pattern, but any simple quilt square would be effective. Since it will be a small block, you will need to avoid the more difficult designs. Nine Patch would be a nice choice, as would Shoo Fly or Churn Dash.

   For Courthouse Steps: cut three 1¾-inch squares from fabric D. Cut ¾-inch strips from the quilt-block fabric for "steps." Sew them together into a block. Figure 4–1 shows both the traditional Log Cabin and the Courthouse Steps variation. Take your pick. The only differences are in the length of the strips and the order of their sewing together. The numbers indicate sewing order.

   For Nine Patch, Shoo Fly, and Churn Dash: use the pattern in figure 4–2. Trace each pattern element (square, rectangle, triangle) and add ¼-inch seam allowance on all sides. Tape to sandpaper and cut with paper scissors. Cut pieces as indicated in the figure from the quilt-block fabric.

   To piece the blocks, take a ¼-inch seam throughout. First sew the triangles together along the bias. (Then sew the rectangles together for Churn Dash.) Piece together strips of three, then piece the complete block.

4. Measure the finished size of your small blocks and cut four 2-inch-wide strips to fit from fabric B. Sew them together with the blocks.

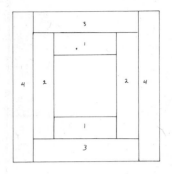

4–1. Courthouse Steps and Log Cabin, step by step.

Courthouse Steps

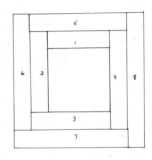

Log Cabin

(for Nine Patch, omit diagonals and alternate squares, checkerboard style)

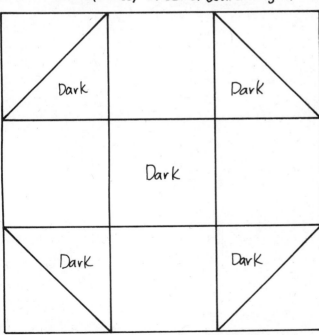

Shoofly: cut   1 square of dark fabric
              4 squares of light fabric
              4 light triangles
              4 dark triangles

4–2. Shoo Fly and Nine Patch variations.

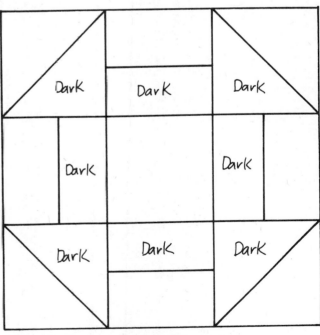

ChurnDash: cut   1 light square
                4 light triangles
                4 light rectangles
                4 dark triangles
                4 dark rectangles

WOMAN'S SIDE-CLOSING DOUBLE-PADDED VEST

4–3. Add strips to vest length.

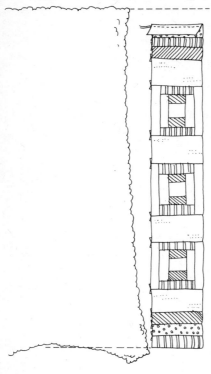

5. Continue adding 2-inch-wide strips (cut from the quilt-block fabric) at top and bottom until you reach the desired length, which is the same as the front vest measurement (fig. 4–3).

6. Cut two strips from fabric B, 2 inches by panel length, and sew them along the sides of the center panel (fig. 4–4). This panel will form one wide central strip on your vest and will be hand quilted later to attach it firmly to the backing and to add interest. Note: this entire panel is not attached to the vest at this point but is a separate piece. It differs from our other string quilted projects in that it is assembled independently and attached later.

7. Measure where you want your front yoke to start. (See step 13 of the *Man's Simple Indoor/Outdoor Vest*, page 24.)

8. Cut strips of fabric A, 2½ inches wide by length determined in step 7. This will use up at least one yard of fabric. Again, differing from other string quilted projects, you will *not* start at the front edge of the vest. Instead, measure how wide your front panel will be with its border and trim strips and allow an extra 2½ inches for strips. Mark a straight line at right angles to the bottom of the vest on the wrap-around front flap and mark with an "invisible" felt-tip pen or with basting stitches.

9. See hints on string quilting in *Beginnings*. Begin sewing your strips along your line. Sew the first strip in place, stitching along the line marked. Continue adding strips until you reach the side seam allowance. If you find you are almost to the edge but with not enough room for a complete strip, try adding a 1-inch strip of fabric C as shown in figure 4–5 to accentuate the seam.

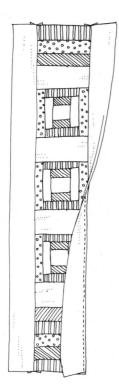

4–4. Add lengthwise strips.

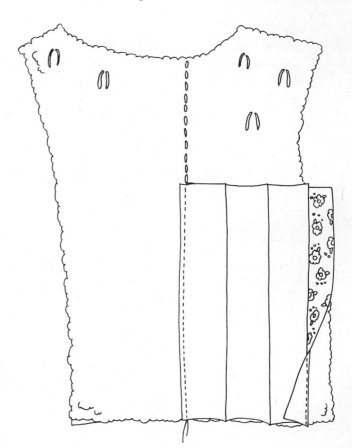

4–5. Piece from mark to side of vest.

10. Making sure to cover the raw edge at the top of your strips, begin adding horizontal strips until you reach the shoulder. Strips will hang over the backing (fig. 4–6).

11. Trim away excess fabric, using the backing as a cutting guide.

12. Cut 1-inch strips of fabric C. This fabric will also be used as the bias binding, so cut only two or three strips by the width of your fabric.

13. Using the angle of the shoulder as a guide, place one strip face down so the upper edge is parallel to and 1¾ inches from the shoulder line as shown. Stitch, taking a ¼-inch seam, and turn toward shoulder.

14. Add a second strip of fabric (one of the quilt-block fabrics would be nice) wide enough to allow for a ¼-inch seam and to cover the shoulder line when turned, as shown. Trim away excess (fig. 4–7).

15. Sew a 1-inch strip of fabric C along the raw edge at the center front of the vest as shown (fig. 4–8).

16. Stitch the center panel (with the blocks) to vest front as if it were just another strip. Turn and press (fig. 4–9).

17. Add another 1-inch strip of fabric C. Then add another of the fabric used in step 14 to reach the edge of the vest front (fig. 4–10). Trim away excess, using backing as a guide.

18. There is no need for the fancy panel on the narrower, under flap (the left side of vest). Simply start the vertical strips at the outer edge and continue until you reach the side. Add trim piece to match the other side.

19. Continue yoke and shoulder detail as on the vest front.

20. For the vest back, cut strips of various widths from 1 inch to 2 inches. Cut one strip from fabric D. Cut these strips 3 inches long.

21. Measure to find the center of the back and the yoke line. Mark with your felt-tip or with basting stitches directly on the batting.

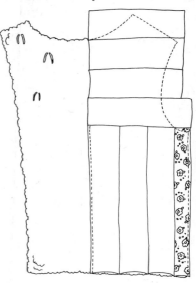

4–6. Yoke strips to shoulder.

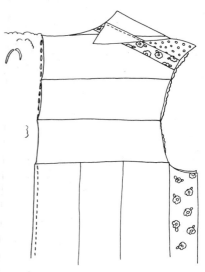

4–7. Shoulder decorations.

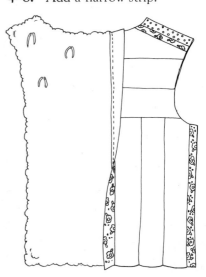

4–8. Add a narrow strip.

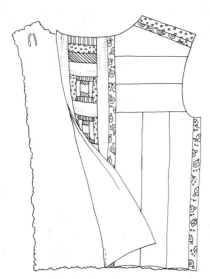

4–9. Add pieced center panel.

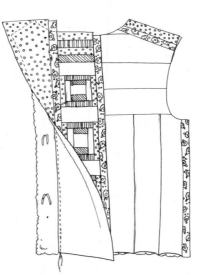

4–10. Finish and trim, using backing as a cutting guide.

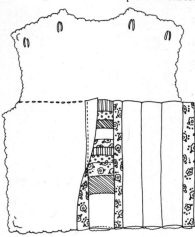

4–11. Center "stack" and string quilt to sides.

22. Pin one of the 3-inch pieces of fabric so it is centered on the middle line. I started at the bottom with a piece of fabric A, 5½ inches by 3 inches, but you may prefer to use thin strips throughout. Sew along the bottom edge, then add strips, sewing through all layers until you reach the yoke marking. You will have a "stack" of strips up the center of the back.

23. Add strips of fabric C, 1 inch wide, to enclose raw edges on both sides of the stack. Add strips of fabric A, 2½ inches wide, until you reach the sides of the vest (fig. 4–11).

24. To define the yoke, sew a 1-inch strip of fabric C along the horizontal line, making sure to cover all the raw edges of the vertical strips.

25. Add a 2-inch strip of fabric D, then a 1-inch strip of fabric C. Add 2½-inch strips of fabric A until you reach the shoulder line (fig. 4–12).

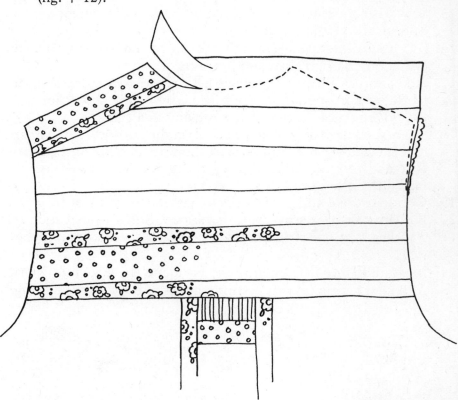

4–12. Finish string piecing to neck and trim.

26. Trim as usual, using backing as a guide.

27. Use the same trim for the back shoulders as you did on the front pieces. (See steps 13 and 14.)

28. Edgestitch around body pieces to hold all layers in place. Trim away any remaining batting and fabric that stick out beyond the backing fabric.

29. Assemble vest by pinning right sides together and taking ⅝-inch seams at sides and shoulders.

30. Bind seams with purchased bias tape or use one of the other seam finishes taught in *Beginnings*.

31. Cut your own bias tape, following the instructions in *Beginnings*. Bind all edges of the vest, including armholes.

32. Try vest on and pin shut. Determine where you need fasteners. Pin on Velcro dots and sew in place.

33. Cut two strips of fabric C, each 2 by 18 inches, for tie. Fold right

sides of each strip together lengthwise and sew across one end and down the length. Turn right side out. Turn under raw end and blindstitch in place as shown in figure 4–13.

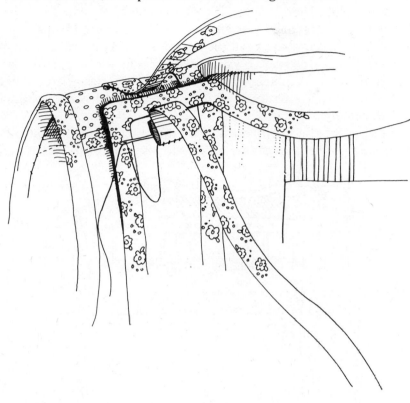

4–13. Blindstitch ties in place.

34. Hand quilt (see section on hand quilting in *Beginnings*) front panel as shown, to contain excess puffiness and to add interest (fig. 4–14).

4–14. Hand quilt center panel.

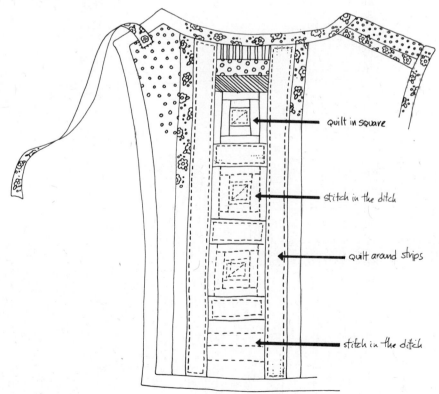

quilt in square

stitch in the ditch

quilt around strips

stitch in the ditch

The Personal Touch

You might prefer to omit the center panel and play up the yoke with strips (fig. 4–15). A more utilitarian-looking vest might appeal to you too.

You might want to try laces and trims. Warmth can be as feminine as it is practical! Use ribbons or embroidered trims in place of fabric strips. Another possibility is a sampler vest utilizing all four suggested blocks—or your own favorite blocks—in the front panel. Experiment with the placement of colors and fabrics. Identically cut blocks can be made to look entirely different by simply changing fabric placement.

Instead of the back "stack" of fabrics, try a medallion block, perhaps a larger version of one of the blocks used on the front panel.

4–15. String quilted yoke.

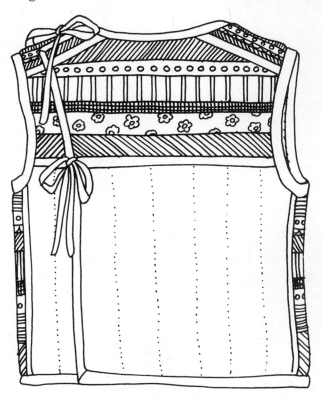

4–16. Sampler vest or frills.

MAN'S EASY-TO-MAKE SHORT ROBE

CATHY JOHNSON

This robe is one of the simplest projects in the book since it utilizes prequilted fabric throughout and requires very little hand work.

Prequilted fabric offers the practicality and warmth of quilting without the time and expertise needed for hand and machine quilting. The fabric can be embellished in any way you like, with extra hand quilting to form a design in the yoke or back, or string quilted fabric for the sleeve trim and yoke.

Making this robe took under three hours, start to finish. The hardest part was finding a print suitable for a man. You may want to use a combination of solid colors. Be sure to buy *reversible* quilted fabric; there should be fabric on both sides of the batting rather than fabric on one side and a lightweight tricot lining on the other. The yardages listed are for a medium-sized man.

As you can see in the photo in the color section, the robe is almost smoking-jacket length, but you can make it longer for greater warmth, if you wish.

Materials

- □ man's simple kimono pattern
- □ fabric A: 2½ yards of reversible prequilted fabric (for body)
- □ fabric B: 1½ yards of contrasting fabric (for pocket band and yoke and sleeve trim)
- □ one spool of thread to match color of fabric A
- □ one spool of thread to match color of fabric B
- □ two packages of wide bias tape in a contrasting color (to cover outside seams)
- □ two packages of wide bias tape to match color of fabric B
- □ one package of hem tape

Directions

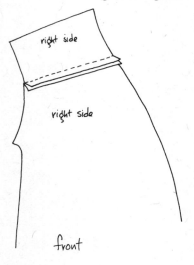

5–1. Sew yoke to robe body, wrong sides together.

1. Lay your pattern pieces out flat and plan the contrasting areas. Most men's kimono patterns will have a cutting line for a shorter-length robe. If this line is at the length you desire, use it. If not (or if the pattern has no short version), measure from shoulder to projected hem length. Make a line parallel to the hem at this point and cut away excess pattern.
2. To make yoke pattern pieces, measure 4 inches down from the shoulder seam on the robe front and robe back pattern pieces and cut pattern apart at that line. Save the strips you cut away. To make pattern piece for sleeve contrast band, cut 4 inches off the bottom of the sleeve pattern.
3. Pin robe front, robe back, and sleeve pattern pieces to fabric A. Add ½-inch seam allowance to top of front and back and to bottom of sleeve. Cut.
4. Pin yoke front, yoke back, and sleeve band pattern pieces to fabric B. Add ½-inch seam allowance to bottom of yokes and to top of sleeve band. Cut.
5. Cut one piece of fabric A, 4 inches by 2 yards, for belt.
6. With *wrong sides together*, stitch robe fronts to yoke fronts, taking a ½-inch seam. Trim seam to ¼ inch and press toward bottom of robe (fig. 5–1).

7. Pin contrasting bias tape over seams and edgestitch in place (fig. 5-2).
8. Repeat steps 6 and 7 for robe back and yoke backs.
9. For pockets, measure 2 inches down from top of pattern piece and cut along this line. Using the larger piece, cut two pockets from fabric A. Using the smaller piece, cut two pocket bands from fabric B.
10. Turn seam allowance to wrong side on three edges of pocket and press (fig. 5-3).
11. Pin pocket band to pocket, with right sides together; open pocket seam allowances to match edges. Stitch, taking a ½-inch seam. Zigzag along raw edge of band (fig. 5-4). Press seam toward band.

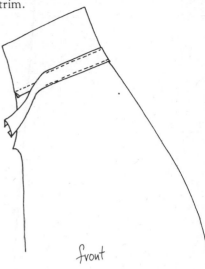

5-2. Cover seam with bias tape trim.

front

5-3. Press under seam allowance.

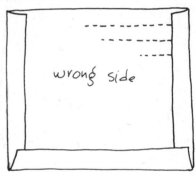

wrong side

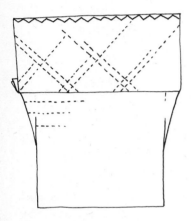

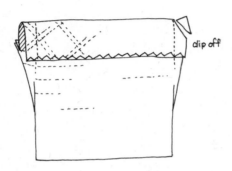

clip off

5-4. Sew band to pocket.

5-5. Clip corners and turn.

12. Fold band to front of pocket, aligning raw edge and pocket/band seam. Stitch band, using the pressed fold line as a guide (fig. 5-5). Clip as shown and turn right side out. Press flat. Edgestitch pocket in place on robe front.
13. Sew shoulder seams, *wrong* sides together. Trim to ¼ inch and cover with contrasting bias tape (fig. 5-6).
14. Sew sleeve bands to sleeves as you did for the yokes and cover with contrasting bias tape.

5-6. Sew shoulder seams and cover with bias tape.

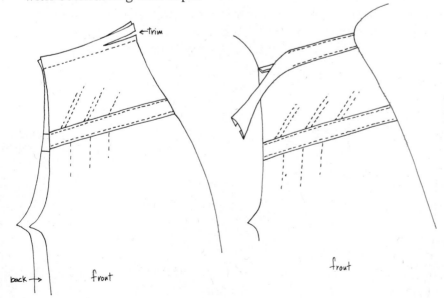

←trim

back→   front

front

MAN'S EASY-TO-MAKE SHORT ROBE

15. Sew sleeves to body, again with the *wrong* sides together. Trim seam to ¼ inch and press toward sleeve. Cover with contrasting bias tape (fig. 5–7).

5–7. Sew sleeves to body and finish with tape.

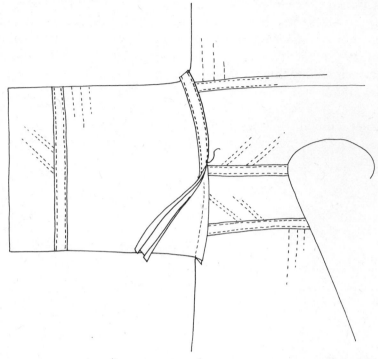

16. With the *right* sides of the fabric together, sew side seams and sleeves in one continuous seam. Bind with the matching bias tape for a finished look.

17. Use the matching bias tape to finish sleeve edges and lower hem. Either bind or turn back and hem.

18. Cut the front-neck band from fabric B. Make center seam according to pattern instructions and press open. Press under ⅝ inch on unnotched side of band.

19. Pin *right* side of band to the inside of the robe, matching band seam and the center of the back-neck edge. Stitch, taking a ½-inch seam. There will be ½ inch of band below the front of the robe on both sides.

20. Turn band back and stitch across lower edge as shown. Grade seam allowances to reduce bulk. Clip corner and turn band. Press along fold line, enclosing raw edges (fig. 5–8).

5–8. Band finish detail.

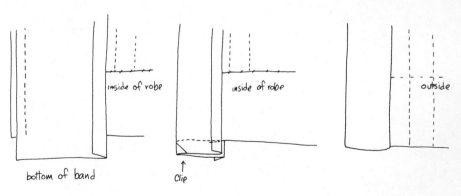

inside of robe   inside of robe   outside

bottom of band   Clip

21. Pin edge of band in place, covering seam, and topstitch in place. A second line of topstitching may be added.

22. Sew across ends and along edges of belt leaving 4 inches open in the middle to turn the belt. Clip corners, turn, and press. Hand stitch opening shut.

Make your own string quilted fabric for yoke and sleeve trim. Try paisleys or plaids with a solid-color body fabric (fig. 5–9).

The Personal Touch

5–9. String quilted yoke and sleeve trim.

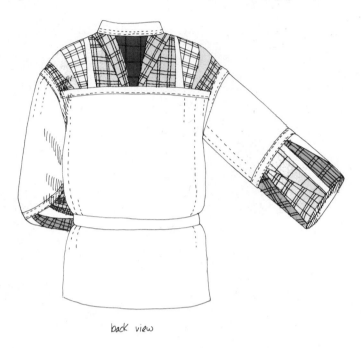

back view

For a simple and subtle effect, hand or machine stitch a design right over the commercial quilting of your fabric (fig. 5–10). The robe shown has the ancient yin and yang symbol machine quilted on the back. Use your own favorite motif—flying geese, cats, waves—whatever.

5–10. Embellish with your own machine quilted design.

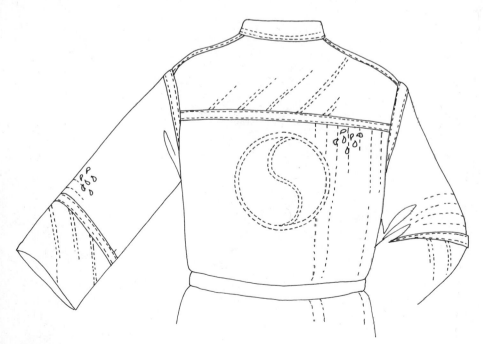

MAN'S EASY-TO-MAKE SHORT ROBE

Man's Easy-to-Make Short Robe; Man's Vest; Warm Winter Slippers

Velvet Evening Vest

Crazy Quilt Victorian Vest

Woman's Floor-length Robe

Sampler Vest

Woman's Lace and Ribbon Jacket

Woman's String Quilted Vest; Movable Mittens

Seminole Shirt; Warm, Padded Vest with Seminole Trim

Doggie Coat; Woman's Side-closing Double-padded Vest

Whitework Tabard Vest; Flower Baby Bunting

Nora's Rainbow Vest; Molly's Dream Jumper; Rachel's Machine-appliquéd Vest

Rich Turkish Coat

WOMAN'S FLOOR-LENGTH ROBE

CATHY JOHNSON

Here's the solution to a chilly morning wake-up call—a floor-length, quilted robe. This snuggly robe is made of prequilted fabric, but string quilted embellishments make it your own and add both warmth and beauty to the finished garment. I am often tempted to wear mine as a coat!

The extra padding in the string quilted areas increases warmth where you need it most. (It's a known fact that we lose a great deal of our body's heat through the head and upper parts of the body.)

Choose a simple, wrap-front robe pattern. The one I used had set sleeves, a choice not usually recommended for quilted clothing. However, since prequilted fabric is a bit lighter in weight and the closeness of the stitching rows holds fabric and backing together tightly, the set sleeves were not really a problem.

You'll need reversible prequilted fabric for this robe. As you can see in the photograph in the color section, the fabric I used was solid on one side and print on the other—an easy, exciting lining. Cotton or polycotton is a good choice for the other fabrics. The yardages that follow are for a medium-sized robe.

Materials

- robe pattern
- fabric A: 3½ yards of reversible prequilted fabric (60 inches wide)
- fabric B: ½ yard of print fabric
- fabrics C: ¼ yard *each* of four different print fabrics
- fabric D: ¼ yard of solid fabric (for pocket backing)
- ½ yard of bonded quilt batting
- one package of double fold bias tape to contrast with color of fabric A
- three packages of wide bias tape in the same color as the double fold tape
- two packages of wide bias tape in a color that harmonizes with fabrics C
- two spools of thread to match colors of bias tape
- three round buttons
- tissue paper

Directions

1. Make any necessary adjustments to your paper pattern, lengthening or shortening skirt or sleeves as needed. Since edges of the finished garment will be bound with bias tape, omit facing and hem allowances.

2. Lay out your main pattern pieces on fabric A, using the cutting guide enclosed with your pattern. Cut. Cut two pocket backing pieces from fabric D (fig. 6–1). Tip: sharp shears are a big help with quilted fabrics, as you are dealing with many layers where the fabric is doubled.

3. You need to plan out your design for the string quilted trim. Lay out your pattern pieces on tracing paper as shown (fig. 6–2). Draw around the pieces, then draw the basic shape of the areas to be quilted on the tracing paper. Cut out new pattern pieces along these lines.

6–1. Cutting pattern for robe pocket.

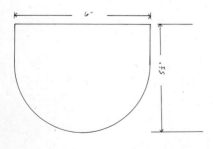

6-2. Plan areas to be string quilted.

area to be quilted

area to be quilted

area to be quilted

cut tracing paper pattern along this line

cut tracing paper pattern along this line

4. There are two methods to use in making the master pattern—either measure everything carefully and draw it on the tracing paper or fold the tracing paper to the desired design. Each section can then be carefully labeled. Regardless of which method you use, make another tissue pattern exactly like the first, transferring section markings. Label the sections exactly like your master pattern and cut apart along fold lines (fig. 6–3).

6-3. Make a master pattern, plus one to cut apart.

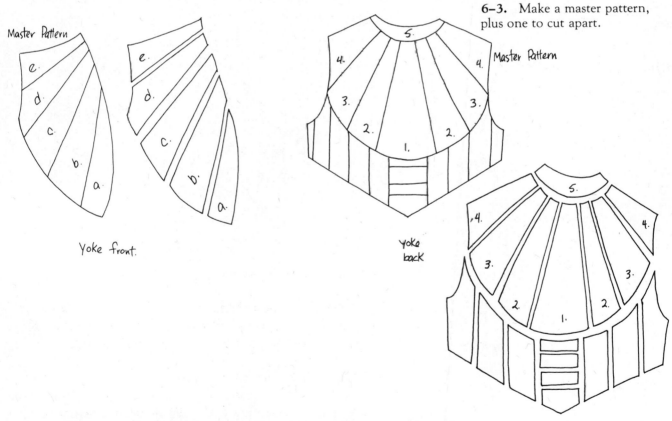

Master Pattern

e. d. c. b. a.

e. d. c. b. a.

Yoke front.

Master Pattern

5. 4. 4. 3. 3. 2. 2. 1.

yoke back

5. 4. 4. 3. 3. 2. 2. 1.

5. Cut three pieces of batting, using your master tissue paper pattern and allowing ½-inch all around.

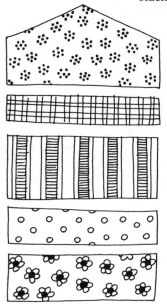

6-4. Central chevron and fabric "stack."

6. Use the cut master patterns as a guide to cut your fabric prints. Allow ¼-inch seam allowance on all sides. Cut two each of the front for a symmetrical look.

7. Using the cut master patterns as a guide and adding ¼-inch seam allowance to all sides, cut one of piece #1 and one of piece #5 from fabric B. Then cut two each of the remaining pieces on the curved yoke back.

8. Cut strips 2 inches wide by varying lengths for the striped bottom area and cut strips 4 inches wide by varying lengths for the stack in the middle of the design. Cut the chevron 4 inches wide as shown (fig. 6–4).

9. Sew the stack of 4-inch strips together, taking ¼-inch seams. End with the chevron. Press all seams down toward the chevron.

10. Attach batting to the *right* side of the robe back with tailor tacks. Baste along seam lines and transfer markings with yellow tailor's chalk.

11. Review string quilting tips in *Beginnings*. Position the stack on the batting; make sure the point of the chevron is at the middle of the back. Pin and stitch along both sides as shown in figure 6–5.

6-6. Add strips to edge.

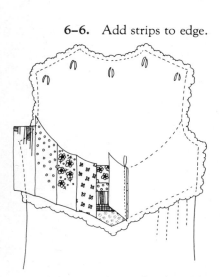

6-7. See step 13.

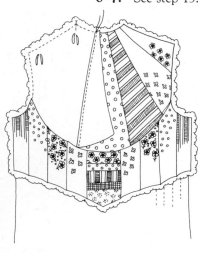

mark with tailor's chalk

baste batting in place

right side of robe fabric

6-5. Position batting and fabric strips on robe back.

12. Following the master pattern, lay two 2-inch strips over the chevron, stitch, and press. Continue until you reach the edges. I like to alternate colors for good contrast and visual interest (fig. 6–6).

13. Center piece #1 just over the chevron stack and stitch in place (fig. 6–7). Do not worry about the raw edges where the fabrics meet; they will be covered with bias tape. Continue adding pieces #2, 3, and 4 until you reach the edges. Add additional strips if you come out short—creative adaptability *is* a necessity in sewing.

14. Position piece #5 as indicated on the master pattern and stitch in place.

15. Machine baste through all layers—string quilting, batting, and backing—along the edges. Trim away excess batting and fabric, using robe back as a cutting guide.

16. Trim away excess fabric where the two design elements touch and cover raw edges with harmonizing wide bias tape, as shown in figure 6–8. Add bias tape to cover raw edges at the bottom of your design as well.

17. Attach batting to *right* side of front yokes with tailor tacks and mark the actual area of the yoke edge directly on the batting with yellow tailor's chalk. Line up pieces with the chalked line and sew along outside edge as shown.

18. Follow master pattern and continue adding pieces in order until you reach the shoulder seam. Machine baste and trim away excess batting and fabric as in step 15 (fig. 6–9).

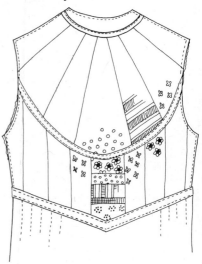

6–8. Trim and cover raw edges with bias tape.

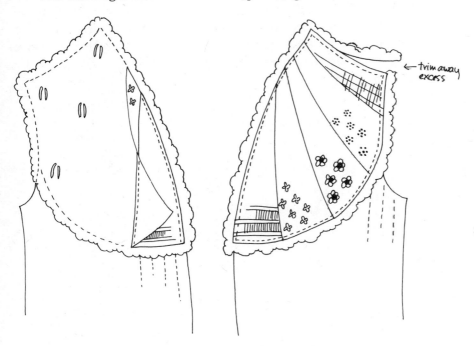

6–9. Finish front yoke and trim excess batting.

19. For the pockets, transfer pocket pattern to tissue paper and make a master pattern of wedge-shaped pieces similar to that of the yoke. Cut pieces from print fabrics. String quilt to pocket backing (fig. 6–10). No batting is necessary.

20. Bind the curved edge with harmonizing wide bias tape, then bind the top as shown. Sew in place on robe front, stitching in the ditch as shown in figure 6–11.

6–10. Pocket detail.

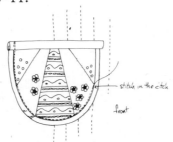

6–11. Bind pocket and stitch in the ditch to robe front.

6–12. Add sleeve trim.

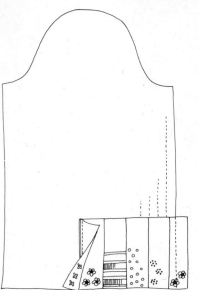

21. Sew robe fronts to robe back, following pattern instructions. Bind seams with the double fold bias tape.
22. Extra batting is not necessary for the sleeve trim but may be used if desired. Cut strips 2 inches by 5 inches from your printed fabrics. Pin a strip in the center of your sleeve (raw edges matching) and stitch down on both sides. Add strips until you reach the seam allowances (fig. 6–12).
23. Cover raw edges at top of trim with harmonizing bias tape.
24. Sew sleeve seams. Bind seams with double fold bias tape.
25. Sew sleeves into robe, following pattern instructions. Bind seam with double fold tape for a finished look inside your garment.
26. Bind all remaining edges (bottom of sleeves, front, neck, and hem of robe) with contrasting wide bias tape. Finish by hand on the inside, or topstitch on the outside by machine.
27. To make simple closures, cut a 12-inch strip of wide bias tape. Fold in half lengthwise and edgestitch shut. Cut into pieces 3½ inches long. Fold each piece to a point, as shown in figure 6–13. Hand stitch the point in place. Then, allowing room for the button, stitch the ends together tightly. Whipstitch in place on the underside of robe front. Sew buttons in place on opposite front.

6–13. Robe closures.

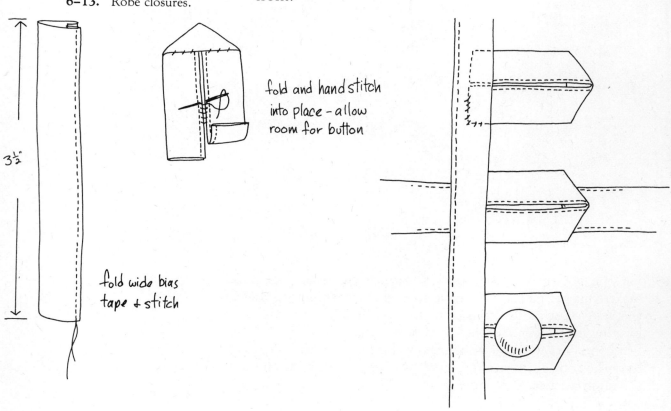

$3\frac{1}{2}$"

fold wide bias tape + stitch

fold and hand stitch into place – allow room for button

A wedge design on the sleeves would be pretty. Or try omitting the yoke design and do a string quilted border all around the robe for striking results.

Quilted velvet is now available in the stores. Try using velvets, velveteens (perhaps printed velveteens), satins, and taffetas for a really elegant look. Dry-clean only, of course.

A beautifully exotic robe could be made by combining appliqué and a carefully planned pattern of hand quilting (fig. 6–14). Choose frog closures for this robe and see if you can find some lovely antique buttons.

The Personal Touch

6–14. An exotic variation.

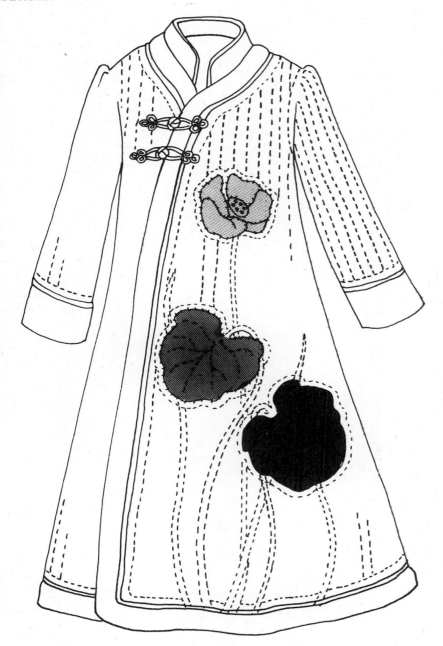

WHITEWORK TABARD VEST

CATHY JOHNSON

The tabard is a one-piece style that probably has its earliest origins in prehistoric man's skin garments. Although this particular design has a front opening, the basic tabard has a hole for the head and drapes over the wearer's shoulders. Depending on fabric and color choice, a tabard looks good with both casual clothes and more dressy outfits. I wear this one with baggy pants or a silky skirt.

When designing this garment, I considered using a botanical pattern and even quilted balloons before deciding to pay homage to my other love, cats. Since this fondness is shared by a lot of people these days, I have included the sketch of my quilting design. Any motif could be substituted—a traditional pattern or one of your own.

The geometric border sets off the fat, puffy cats and is inspired by Japanese sashiko-style quilting. This subtle, white-on-white quilting is often called "whitework." Unbleached muslin is a great fabric choice for this vest, but polycotton will do. Or try silk for a more elegant look.

Materials

- 2½ yards of white or off-white fabric
- 1 yard of print fabric
- ½ yard of bonded quilt batting
- 6 yards of ¼-inch polyester cord
- 6 yards of ½-inch polyester cord (optional)
- one spool of white or off-white thread
- one spool of white or off-white quilting thread

Directions

1. Determine desired vest length by measuring the person for whom the vest is being made from back to front, as shown in figure 7–1. A waist-length vest would be approximately 40 inches; a hip-length one, 47 inches. Also measure shoulder width, as shown.

7–1. Determine tabard measurements.

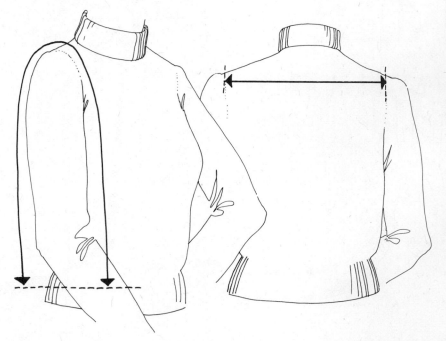

2. Lay out solid fabric and mark measurements or make a paper pattern to work from. Cut out this rectangle.

3. To cut the tabard shape, round the corners. Mark the neckline and center front openings as shown in figure 7–2. The neckline opening should intersect the lengthwise measurement. Cut along these lines.

4. Cut lining from print fabric, using the vest top (solid fabric) or the paper pattern. Cut batting to the basic tabard shape, adding ½ inch to all sides of pattern.

5. Enlarge the quilting pattern (fig. 7–3) or draw a design of your own. With the vest opened out flat, transfer the design to the right side of the solid fabric. Use a 2H pencil, a quilting pencil, or a washable felt-tip pen (follow manufacturer's directions for use and removal).

6. Place lining right side down on a flat surface. Place batting on lining, then cover with solid fabric, right side up. Pin around the edges.

7. Baste edges together and remove pins. Then baste through all layers from the neckline out to distribute the fabric evenly over the batting. Try on (or have the recipient try on) the garment at this point to check fit and size. Make any necessary adjustments *before* starting the hand quilting. (I had designed mine with an extended shoulder line, and when I tried it on I looked very much like a pro linebacker. I decided to cut away the extended shoulders and make the sides straight!)

8. Review the quilting tips in *Beginnings*. Hand quilt along drawn lines.

9. Following the instructions in *Beginnings* (pages 13–14), cut bias tape from the solid fabric as follows: 8 yards 3½ inches wide and 6 yards 2 inches wide. Fold the 3½-inch tape in half lengthwise and press. Leave the 2-inch tape unfolded.

10. To make the ties, use the 2-inch tape and the ¼-inch cord. Cut cord twice as long as required. Sew fabric over cord as shown, using a zipper foot to allow you to sew close to the cording (fig. 7–4). Be sure to sew a little "turning ease" into the end as shown in the illustration. Trim excess seam to ¼ inch and turn tie right side out, pulling the bias back over the cord. It may help to dampen your fingers as you work the fabric over the cording, to give a bit of grip.

7–2. Cut from those measurements, curving corners. Make neck opening.

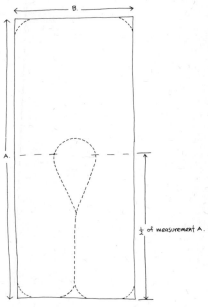

¼ of measurement A.

7–3. My quilting design. Enlarge if desired and follow lines with fine quilting stitches.

7–4. Tabard ties padded with cord. Allow some turning ease.

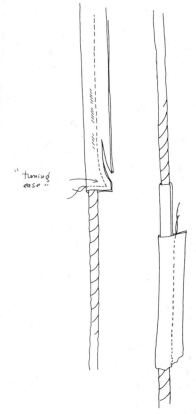

"turning ease"

11. Cut four pieces of fabric-covered cord 9 inches long and cut four pieces 14 inches long. Make Chinese ball knots in one end (fig. 7–5), making sure the cord end is enclosed *inside* the knot.

7–5. Chinese ball knots are simple.

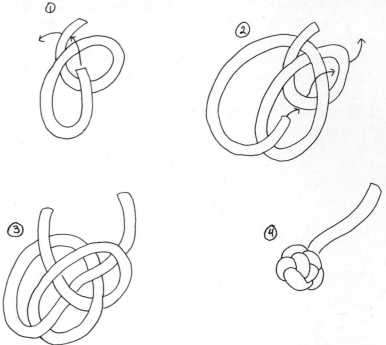

12. Pin in place as shown on vest top (fig. 7–6). The 9-inch pieces are for the sides; the 14-inch ties are for the vest front.

13. Sew the 3½-inch bias binding in place around the vest, taking a ½-inch seam (fig. 7–7). Work turning ease into outside corners as you sew around curves by pushing some extra bias under the pressure foot of your machine.

14. Turn bias to inside and slipstitch in place. For a plump effect, enclose ½-inch cord as you sew.

15. Tie side cords and your vest is finished.

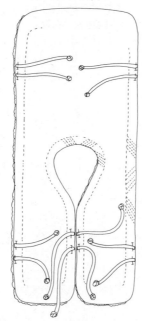

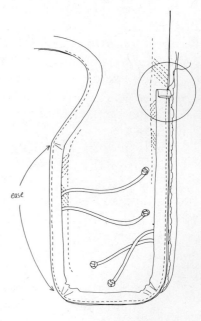

7–6. Tie placement.

7–7. Bind edges, catching ties in seam.

If you want your design to stand out more, try using quilting thread in a contrasting color. Real sashiko quilting is often done with a heavy thread that would make your design pop out even more.

An overall quilted design like the clamshell (fig. 7–8) would be a beautiful touch—or consider a traditional pattern like the feather wreath or sheaf of wheat (fig. 7–9).

If you have carefully hidden your knots it will be reversible. Wear your vest inside out. It can even be worn backwards for a whole new look (fig. 7–10).

A more casual effect can be gained by using a calico or other patterned binding.

For an easier garment, omit cording and just bind with bias strips. Fold and edgestitch bias for ties.

The Personal Touch

7–8. An overall clamshell design.

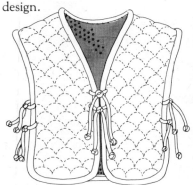

7–9. A traditional pattern.

7–10. Try it inside out!

FLOWER BABY BUNTING

Bye baby bunting. Daddy may have gone a-hunting for rabbit skin, but he won't find a sweeter sleeper to wrap his baby bunting in. Extra-thick batting keeps baby bundled safely away from winter winds.

This sleeper is based on a Simplicity pattern that lends itself to a number of interpretations. It is fast and easy, a satisfying project. I have used a heavy zipper to form the flower stem, and directions are included for sewing it in place so that the zipper will remain a design element. For another interpretation, insert the zipper according to manufacturer's directions.

The pattern calls for three parallel lines of quilting down the back to hold everything together, but it is more fun to branch out and design your own. I made a design of hearts meeting at their points.

The yardages that follow are for a six-month size. Choose a polycotton for washing ease.

Materials

- bunting pattern
- fabric A: ½ yard of solid fabric
- fabric B: ¼ yard of solid fabric in a contrasting color
- fabric C: ¼ yard of solid fabric in a darker shade of the color of fabric B
- fabric D: 1¼ yards of striped fabric in matching colors
- 1¼ yards of flannel in any color
- 1¼ yards of extra-thick bonded quilt batting
- scrap of lightweight batting or flannel
- heavy-duty zipper to match color of fabric B, 23 inches long
- one package of quilt binding to match color of fabric A
- one package of wide rickrack to match color of fabric B
- 1 yard of grosgrain ribbon (for ties)

Directions

1. Using your pattern, cut one bunting shape each from fabric D, flannel, and batting.
2. Place flannel on a flat surface, right side *down*. Place fabric D on top, right side *up*, with batting in between. Pin all around the edges.
3. Machine baste around edges, ⅜ inch from edge.
4. Enlarge the heart pattern to suit your needs (fig. 8–1) or fold and cut a heart shape from heavy paper. Trace around the shape on the back of the bunting to mark quilting lines, as shown, and stitch through all layers by machine (fig. 8–2).
5. Cut a strip of fabric B 3 inches by the width of the bunting bottom and stitch to the sleeper top.
6. Cut a strip of fabric C 2 inches by the width of the sleeper and press under ¼ inch along one edge.
7. Place strip right side down over the top edge of the first strip, folded edge to the bottom (fig. 8–3). Sew in place and press upward to cover edge.

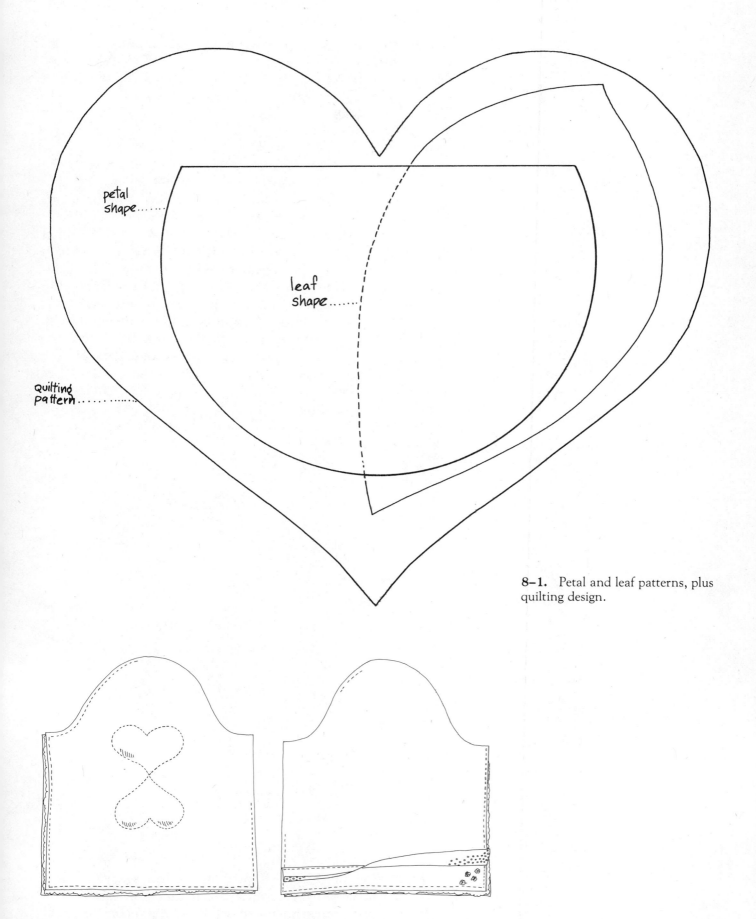

petal
shape......

leaf
shape......

quilting
pattern......

8–1. Petal and leaf patterns, plus quilting design.

8–2. Trace hearts onto fabric and quilt.

8–3. Add bands to sleeper bottom.

8. Hold or pin rickrack in place as shown and stitch down folded edge to bunting.

9. Cut four leaf shapes (see fig. 8–2) from fabric C and two from a scrap of lightweight batting or flannel.

10. Pin two leaves, right sides together, and place one batting piece on top. Sew around outside with a ⅜-inch seam, leaving 2 inches open to turn leaves. Repeat for second leaf.

11. Trim away excess batting and seam allowances and clip the curves and points. Turn leaves right side out, press, and slip-stitch opening. Topstitch ¼ inch from the edge all around, and sew down the middle of each leaf for the leaf vein.

12. Enlarge the petal shape (see fig. 8–2) or draw around a 6½-inch dessert plate to make your own. Use the pattern to cut eighteen petals from fabric A. Put them together in twos, right sides together, and sew around the curve with a ⅜-inch seam. Clip curves, trim excess fabric and batting, turn, and press petals.

13. Evenly space petals around the hood opening of the bunting, as shown in figure 8–4, on the right side of the fabric. It is easier to get them evenly spaced if you center the first one, then pin the two on each end. Pin another petal between these, then fill in with remaining four petals. You may wish to baste them in place once they are spaced (fig. 8–4).

8–4. Space petals evenly around curve.

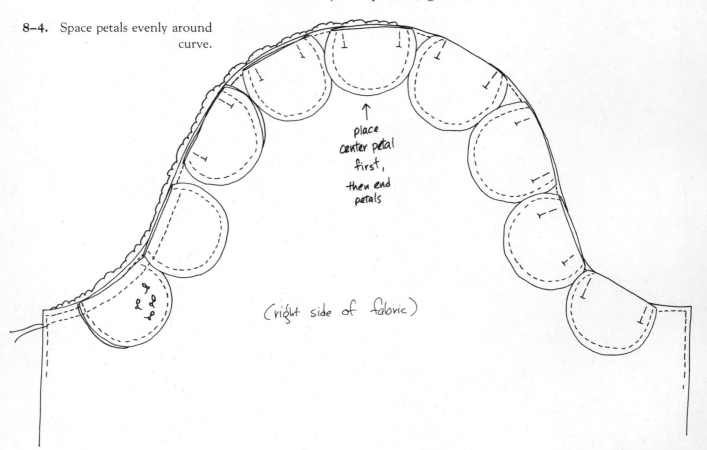

place
center petal
first,
then end
petals

(right side of fabric)

14. To insert zipper, place it, face down, on left front seam allowance (fig. 8–5). Fold down top edge of zipper tape and catch in the stitches as you sew near the outside edge of the tape. Turn back and topstitch. You may need to open or shut the zipper to facilitate sewing past the zipper pull.

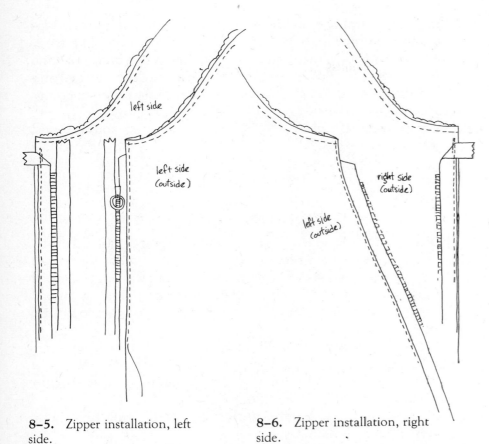

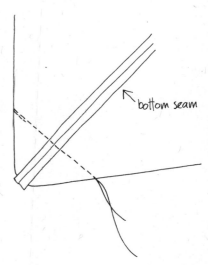

8-7. Box corners as shown.

8-5. Zipper installation, left side.

8-6. Zipper installation, right side.

15. Open zipper and place the free side down on the right seam allowance. Stitch, catching the folded zipper tape at the top (fig. 8-6). Turn back and topstitch. This zipper application will leave more visible than usual, forming the green "stem."

16. Zip shut, turning bunting wrong side out, and position zipper in the middle of the bunting front. Sew seam, catching to bottom edge of zipper tape in the seam.

17. Box the sleeper corners as shown in figure 8-7. Turn bunting right side out.

18. Slipstitch leaves in place, sewing only the top edge (fig. 8-8). The leaf remains free on the bottom, giving a three-dimensional effect.

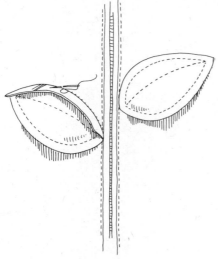

8-8. Attach "leaves" firmly.

FLOWER BABY BUNTING

8–9. Bind edges to form casing for ties.

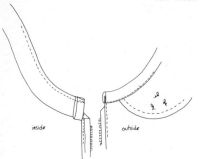

inside   outside

19. Enclose remaining raw edge with quilt binding. (Use wide bias tape or hem tape if quilt binding is not available.) Fold back ⅜ inch at seam allowances on both sides and catch with machine stitches. Bias should be sewn first to the inside, then turned and machine stitched to the outside of the bunting. Leave openings at front edge to form casing (fig. 8–9).
20. Insert grosgrain ribbon in the casing and pull snug around baby's face.

The Personal Touch

8–10. An appliquéd scene.

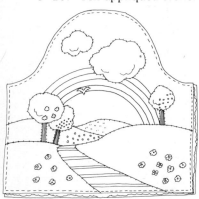

put extra padding in
clouds and trees

Try Prairie Points for petals. Fold a square of fabric diagonally, then bring folded edges to the center or to the side. Experiment with paper squares to find the best size. Sew in place and cut away excess fabric.

Make an appliquéd scene (by hand or machine) before inserting zipper, with hills, rainbows (bias tape makes a good rainbow), and clouds (fig. 8–10).

Turn your bunting into a bunny sleeper. Make it from a soft flannel, add two ears instead of petals, a soft pom-pom "tail," and hugging paws instead of leaves, as shown in figure 8–11. Batting in the ears will help them to stand up.

Elegant all-over quilting turns the bunting into a keepsake. Use a lightweight batting here.

8–11. Bunting variations.

WARM WINTER SLIPPERS

CATHY JOHNSON

These fleece-lined booties were based, very loosely, on an American Indian moccasin design: Apache styling is combined with the western Plains Indians' flat sole for ease of construction. I used a prequilted denim and fleece sewn together. If that particular combination is hard to find, the separate components are not. Simply buy ½ yard each of denim and fleece and space lines of stitching 2 inches apart. You could even stitch fancy diamonds or squares.

These slipper-booties have a small "Dresden Plate" design appliquéd to the toe. You may wish to use something simpler, or perhaps a Pennsylvania Dutch hearts-and-tulips design. The sides can be worn up, for extra warmth, or turned down to show the fleecy lining as a design element. A textured nonskid fabric could be used for the soles, and for extra winter warmth a pair of lambswool innersoles could be inserted.

This slipper is sized for an adult, but it is easy to modify to any size. You may want to make a prototype with leftover scraps of quilted fabric to check for size and fit. I did, and then made some slight changes.

Materials

- ½ yard of prequilted denim/fleece fabric *or* ½ yard *each* of denim and fleece
- ½ yard of print fabric (for bias binding and corded ties)
- 3 yards of ¼-inch polyester cord
- one package of double fold bias tape
- small scraps (for appliqué)
- heavy brown paper

Directions

1. Draw around foot on a piece of heavy paper. Allow ⅜ inch for seams on the sides; add ¾ inch at the heel and ½ inch at the toe for walking ease (fig. 9–1). Cut pattern.

9–1. Sole pattern—draw around foot.

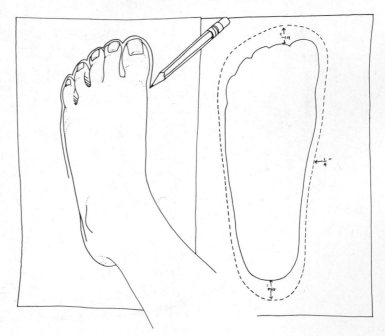

2. For the upper, place sole pattern on paper. Follow the sole's top shape for the toe half, adding about 2½ inches on each side at the center (to allow for instep) and easing to the toe. The tongue should extend almost to the natural heel mark (*not* to the cutting line of the sole) as shown in figure 9–2. Cut pattern.

3. For the heel, measure a rectangle about 6½ inches by length A (fig. 9–3). When sewn, the heel will overlap the upper piece. Round the top edges and cut pattern.

4. Cut slippers from the denim/fleece.

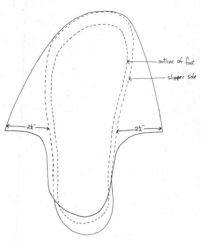

9–2. Upper.

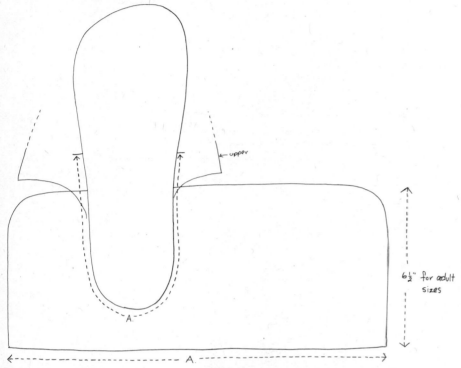

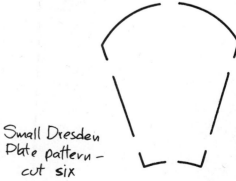

9–3. Heel pattern.

5. Appliqué the upper now, while it is flat and easy to work on. For the Dresden Plate, use the pattern given in figure 9–4. Cut six pieces from your fabric scraps and sew together, taking a ¼-inch seam, to form a half circle. Pin in place on the upper and turn under the edges as you appliqué. There is no need to turn under the straight edge; it will be covered. Repeat for other upper.

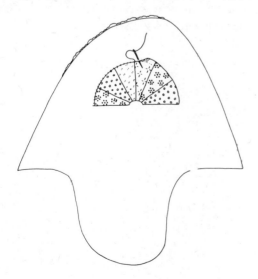

9–4. Appliqué upper with Dresden Plate or design of your choice.

Small Dresden Plate pattern — cut six

9–5. Cover center of appliqué.

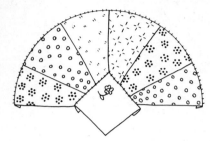

6. Fold a small square of scrap fabric to cover any exposed raw edges in the center and appliqué in place (fig. 9–5).
7. Cut a strip of fabric 2 inches wide and press under ¼ inch along one edge. Cover the raw edge of the appliqué and stitch. Turn back and press. Stitch in place.
8. Center a strip of double fold bias tape on fabric strip and edge-stitch both sides (fig. 9–6). Trim along sole.

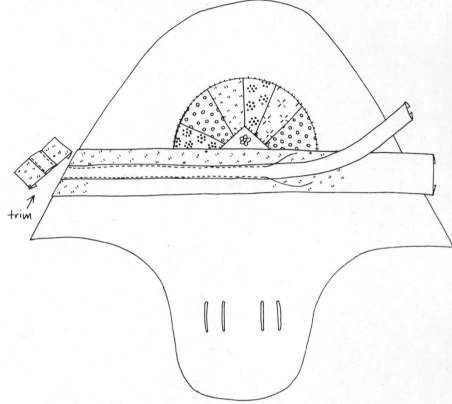

9–6. Add trim strips.

9. Make bias tape from the print fabric (see the section on seam finishes in *Beginnings*). A 16-inch square should make enough to bind the slippers. Cut bias 2 inches wide, fold, and press length-wise.
10. Make buttonholes in heel and tongue, spacing them as indicated in figure 9–7.
11. Bind tongue edge of upper by sewing bias to the inside of slipper. Turn to the outside and edgestitch.

9–7. Buttonhole placement.

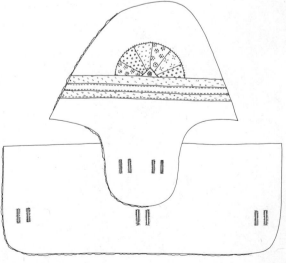

12. Bind upper curved edge of heel as you did the upper.
13. Trim fleece along seam lines to reduce bulk. In other words, give the fleece a "haircut," being careful not to cut into backing.
14. Pin upper in place on sole, fleece sides together. Begin pinning in front, matching the curve of the toe, then continue pinning to the sides. Ease curve into place. Baste and remove pins (fig. 9–8).
15. Clip heel in the center to the seam line as shown. This will allow ease around the curve of the heel. Pin, starting in the middle of the back. (The seam allowance will form a right angle around the heel.) Baste. Machine stitch the three pieces together, taking a ⅜-inch seam.

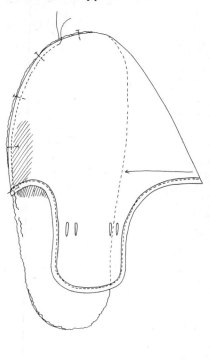

9–8. Stitch upper to sole.

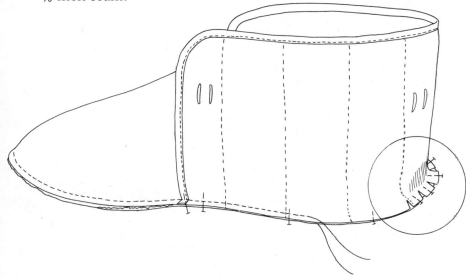

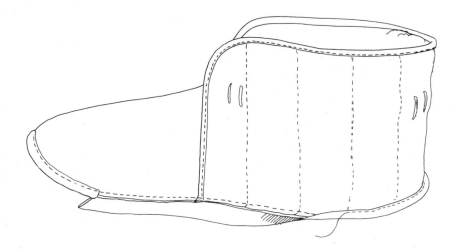

16. Trim away excess seam allowance around sole. You may need to grade seam allowance, especially where the upper and heel pieces overlap.
17. Bind edges of the sole and slipper tops, edgestitching bias on the top side (fig. 9–10).

9–9. Attach heel piece, clipping at heel.

9–10. Bind remaining edges.

18. Make 1-inch-wide bias tape from the print fabric. Cover ¼-inch polyester cording as shown on page 51. Tie ends in knots and thread through buttonholes as shown in figure 9–11.

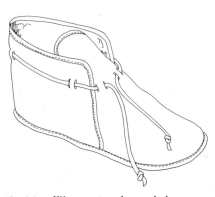

9–11. Weave ties through buttonholes.

The Personal Touch

String quilt your own fabrics for slippers, following the shape of the pieces.

For easier booties, you could use a readymade appliqué and bind with wide bias tape. Omit cord and simply fold and stitch bias tape for ties. Try using rainbow colors of bias tape or use calico tape.

If you do not have a buttonhole option or a buttonhole attachment on your machine, small plastic rings sewn to the outside make an interesting casing for ties. Elastic around the back piece at the ankle plus a ribbon tie make an alternate closure, and for a man's slipper, a tab-and-gripper snap is a good choice (fig. 9–12).

9–12. Slipper options.

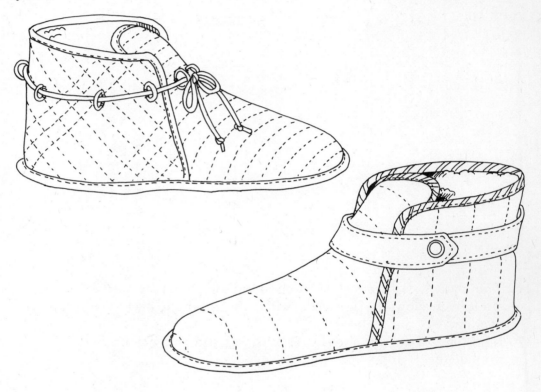

MOVABLE MITTENS

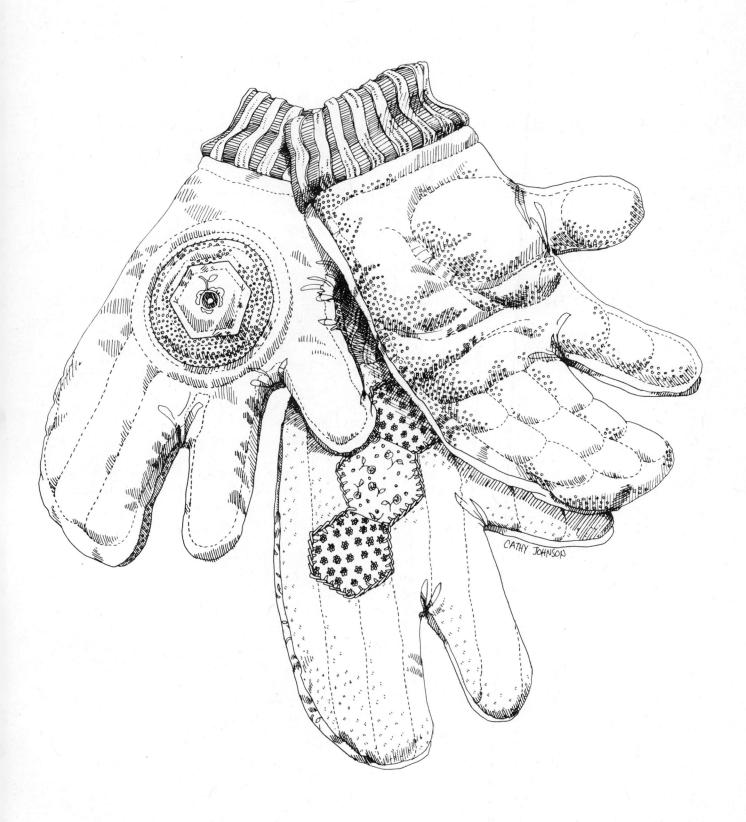

CATHY JOHNSON

Mittens come in many shapes and sizes. Responding to my husband, who asked why mittens couldn't have a free index finger for more flexibility, I decided to make a new type of mitten, a "movable" mitten. The mitten I came up with is handsome and toasty warm—a wonderful conversation starter, too!

The mittens are unconventional (see the color section for a photograph), but somewhat easier to make than the regular three-piece mitten design found in some pattern books. They require no pattern or special expertise. Choose cotton or polycotton for the quilting fabrics and flannel or some other very soft fabric for the backing and lining. If you would like thinner mittens, substitute flannel or scraps from an old, soft blanket for the batting.

Materials

- fabric A: ¼ yard of solid fabric
- fabric B: ¼ yard of calico fabric
- fabric C: ½ yard of flannel (for backing)
- fabric D: ½ yard of flannel (for lining)
- scrap of a different calico fabric
- ½ yard of bonded quilt batting
- length of 6-inch knit ribbing (length will depend on wrist size)

Directions

10-1. See step 1.

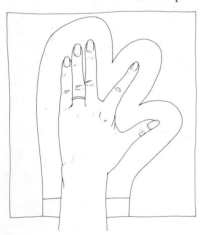

1. Spread out your hand on a sheet of heavy paper and draw around your hand, allowing 1¼ inch all around (fig. 10–1). Cut out shape. (It will look more like a fat oven mitt than a mitten.)
2. Measure a 3-inch circle and a hexagon about half that size on the same heavy paper. Add ¼-inch seam allowance all around and cut out patterns.
3. Cut four rectangles of fabric, each 12 inches by 14 inches—two from fabric A and two from fabric B.
4. Using the same dimensions, cut four rectangles from fabric C and four from batting.
5. Trace mitten shape onto the rectangles cut in step 3, but *do not* cut out yet. Decide which fabric will be for the palm side and which for the back. (You may wish to make a prototype mitten from prequilted fabric to make sure your shape fits and is comfortable.)
6. Using your pattern, cut two circles from contrasting fabric scrap.
7. Using your pattern, cut two hexagons from the fabric you chose for the palm side of the mittens.
8. Clip seam allowances all around circle, as shown in figure 10–2. Clip corners of hexagon. Place your paper pattern on the fabric shapes and press seam allowances over the edge of the back side as shown. Now your seam allowances are neatly pressed and ready for appliqué.
9. Center the circle on the back of the mitten and appliqué in place, using a whipstitch or slipstitch (fig. 10–3).
10. Center hexagon on circle and appliqué in place.

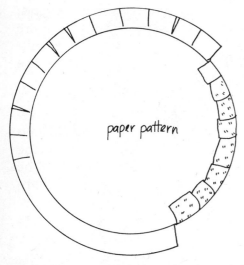

paper pattern

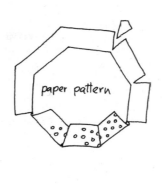

paper pattern

10-2. Cut out and clip circle and hexagon shapes.

10-3. Appliqué to back of mitten shape.

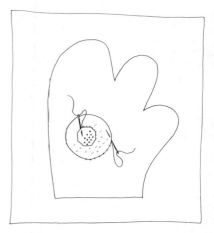

11. Make a "sandwich" of backing, batting, and fabric. Working from the center out, baste in place with contrasting thread, using large running stitches.
12. Baste all around the mitten shape, just inside the cutting line marked on your top fabric, using large stitches.
13. Hand or machine quilt as shown in figure 10–4, or use your own quilting pattern. Keep hand quilting at least ½ inch away from seam line.

10-4. Basting and quilting diagram.

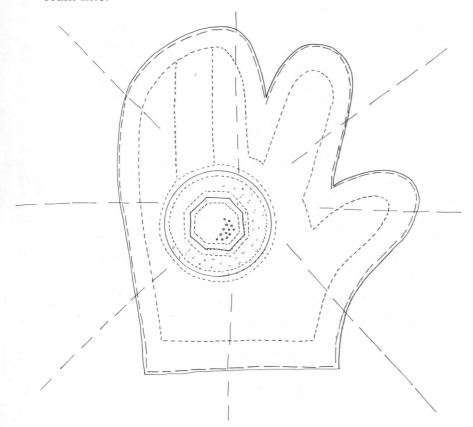

14. Prepare mitten palms the same way, omitting appliqué.
15. Trim away excess fabric and batting at the cutting line. Now you have something with a recognizable shape.

16. Place right sides together, one palm piece with one back. Pin and stitch, as shown in figure 10–5.

10–5. Sew mitten front and back together.

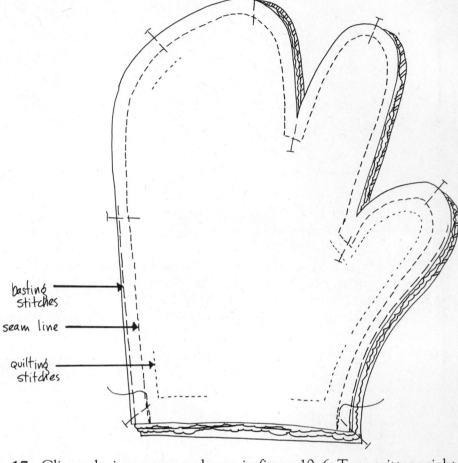

10–6. Clip seams and turn.

basting stitches

seam line

quilting stitches

17. Clip and trim seams, as shown in figure 10–6. Turn mittens right side out.

18. Cut four "hands" from fabric D. Pin and sew, taking a ½-inch seam. Clip to stitching, and trim seams. It is not necessary to clip curves since lining pieces will not be turned.

19. Slip your hand inside lining, then put on mitten to position the lining inside. Pin at side wrist seams.

20. Measure your wrist and cut ribbing to that length. Fold ribbing so side seams are together and sew with a small zigzag stitch (fig. 10–7).

21. Fold seam to the inside so selvage edges are together, as shown in figure 10–8. Pin ribbing to the mitten wrist on the *right* side, with

10–7. Wrist ribbing.

wrist measurement

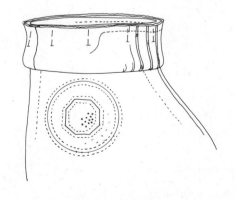

10–8. Sew to mitten, raw edges together.

raw edges matching. Sew with a straight stitch and fold ribbing back over wrist.

String quilt fabric for mittens. For *easy* mittens, try prequilted fabric. Line and add ribbing as before. Appliqué a simple design on the back for fun.

Omit the free finger for even easier mittens. Try binding the raw edge and using elastic 1 inch from the edge instead of ribbing at the wrist (fig. 10–9).

The Personal Touch

10–9. Two variations.

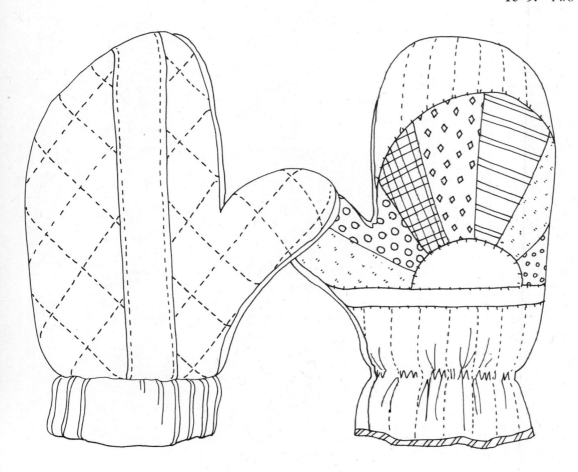

WOMAN'S STRING QUILTED VEST

CATHY JOHNSON

This vest, almost a sleeveless jacket, was my first attempt at quilted clothing and living proof that it is not necessary to begin with an "ABC" project. Sure, I made some mistakes on this one; but I learned a lot, and it's still my favorite article of clothing. I have worn it everywhere—from gallery openings to an interview on television.

The slightly extended shoulder line keeps drafts away, and the stand-up collar protects the neck. If you cannot find a pattern for a vest with a collar, or if you already own a vest pattern you like, simply add a collar from another pattern. Polycottons in delicate prints and soft solids work fine for this project, or choose silks for a very elegant look. I think this vest goes as well with a turtleneck and jeans as it does with a wool skirt and a silk blouse. Turn to the color section for a photograph of this vest.

Materials

- vest pattern (with collar)
- ¼ yard *each* of six different fabrics—solids and prints
- 1½ yards of solid fabric (for backing)
- 1½ yards of bonded quilt batting
- two packages of wide bias tape to match color of one of the prints
- one package of wide bias tape to match color of backing fabric
- two spools of thread (one each to match colors of bias tape)

Directions

1. Lay out pattern and make any necessary adjustments to length, neckline, etc.
2. Cut backing fabric using your pattern, but allowing ½ inch extra at sides.
3. Cut batting, using backing fabric as a pattern. (Make batting an extra ½ inch larger all around.)
4. Review section on string quilting in *Beginnings*. Cut a 4-inch square from one fabric. Cut remaining fabric into strips, some 2 inches wide and some 1 inch. For sawtooth strips, cut two different fabric strips 2 inches wide, then measure again and cut into 2-inch squares. Cut the squares in half diagonally.
5. Attach batting to backing with tailor tacks.
6. Plan where you want your yoke on vest front and back and mark batting with tailor's chalk or basting stitches. On vest back, find the center for the "stack" of fabric strips and mark the same way (fig. 11–1).

11–1. Plan yoke placement.

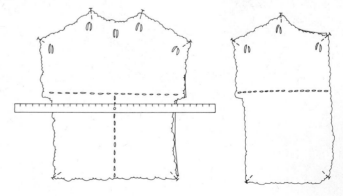

7. Cut some of your strips of fabric into 4-inch lengths; include some 2-inch and some 1-inch strips. Starting with the 4-inch square, sew the stack together along the 4-inch measurement. The stack should be long enough to run from the yoke mark to the bottom of the vest.

8. Place stack on center measurement. There will be 2 inches of fabric to each side of the center line. Stitch down along both sides.

9. For a symmetrical look, place matching 1-inch strips face down on strip as shown. Stitch, turn, and press. Trim two strips down to a width of ¾ inch and string quilt these next. Continue adding fabric strips until you reach the side seams (fig. 11–2).

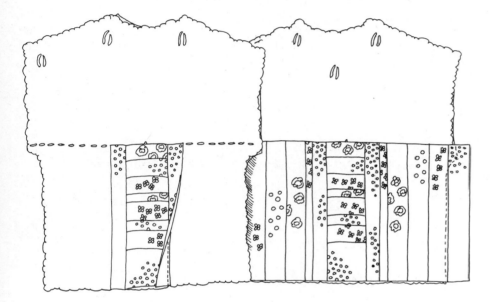

11–2. Add strips on either side of "stack."

10. Cover the raw edges of the vertical strips with a horizontal 2-inch strip.

11. For the sawtooth strip, sew contrasting triangles together along the diagonal as indicated. Sew sixteen squares altogether. Press the seams toward the darker fabric (fig. 11–3).

11–3. Sawtooth strip construction.

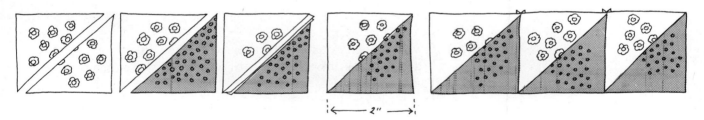

12. I used solid 2-inch squares for greater interest. Choose your central square, then add sawtooth pieces, as shown in figure 11–4. Continue adding solid squares (or more sawtooth pieces, as desired) until you reach width of vest back.

11–4. Finished strip, with plain spacers for interest.

13. Press all seams to one side and string quilt the sawtooth strip to the strip you added in step 10, making sure the center square is

11-5. Finish to neckline and trim away excess.

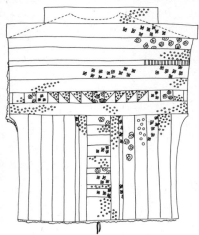

11-6. Shoulder detail.

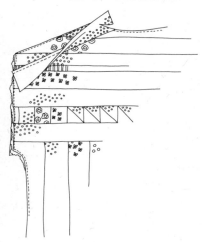

11-7. Front construction.

lined up over the center of the vest. Continue adding strips until you reach the shoulder and neckline seams (fig. 11-5).

14. Using the backing as a guide, trim away all excess fabric.
15. Place a 2-inch strip of fabric, as shown, parallel to and 1¾ inches away from the shoulder line. Stitch, turn, and press, as shown in figure 11-6. Trim away excess fabric.
16. Mark the yoke on the vest front pieces. Beginning at the center front edges of the vest, sew a 2-inch strip in place along the edge. Continue adding strips until you reach the side seams (fig. 11-7). Trim away excess, using the backing as the cutting guide.

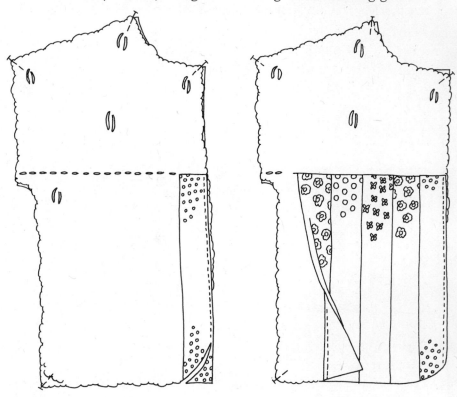

17. Cover the raw edges at the top of the vertical strips with a 2-inch strip.
18. Sew triangles together along the diagonal to make eight sawtooth squares.
19. Sew sawtooth squares together, as shown in figure 11-8. Add 2-inch squares at each end until you reach the width of the vest fronts. (If desired, the sawtooth strips can extend the whole length of the strip.)

11-8. Sawtooth bands for vest front.

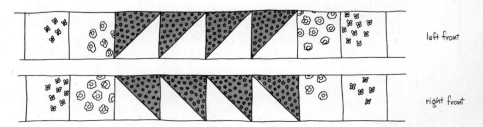

left front

right front

20. String quilt sawtooth strips in place as in step 13.
21. Continue adding strips until you reach the shoulder line. Trim away excess fabric.

22. Finish the shoulders as you did on the vest back (step 15), with fabric strips parallel to the shoulder seam.
23. Edgestitch around all edges of the vest pieces.
24. Join vest fronts and back by placing right sides together and taking a ½-inch seam at sides and shoulders. Be sure that *all* raw edges of your fabric strips are enclosed in the seams.
25. Grade seam allowances to reduce bulk. Bind inside seams with the bias tape that matches the backing.
26. Cut vest collar from backing fabric (follow the vest pattern, or make a straight strip of fabric 2 inches wide by the length of the neck measurement). Cut off corners, as shown in figure 11–9. Cut batting, using this piece as a pattern, and tack into place.

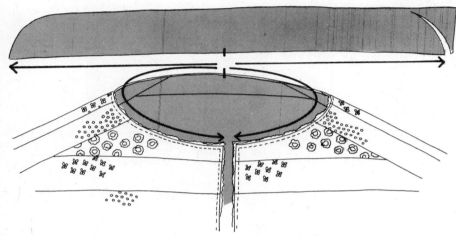

11–9. Cut collar to fit neckline measurements.

27. Find the center of the collar and sew a 2-inch square in place. Continue adding squares to cover the neckband. Trim away excess fabric and batting, using backing as a cutting guide (fig. 11–10).

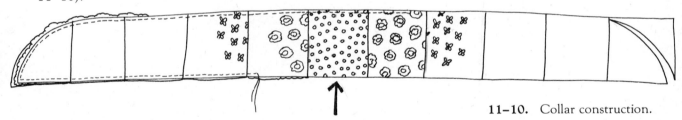

11–10. Collar construction.

28. With right sides together and matching the center of the collar to the middle of the vest, pin neckband to the vest neck. Stitch in place. Bind the raw edge where the two meet with the bias tape you used in step 25 (fig. 11–11).
29. Bind all edges (armholes, bottom, front, and neck band edge) with the bias tape that matches one of the prints.

11–11. Attach collar and bind to finish inside seam.

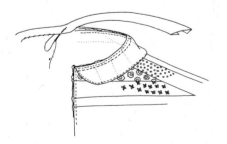

The Personal Touch

11–12. Vest variations.

Try Seminole work for the entire yoke area. A hand-pieced patchwork medallion square could replace the central stack on the back of the vest (fig. 11–12).

Although this vest is designed to be worn open, tie or frog closures could be added.

Use silk or satin for the backing and finish inside seams by hand (see hints in *Beginnings*). The vest will be reversible, with a beautiful patchwork "lining."

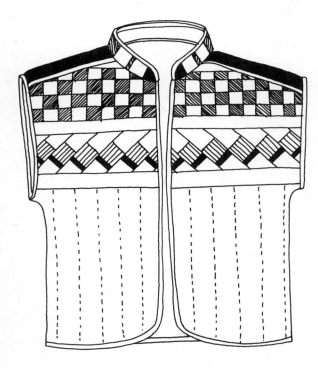
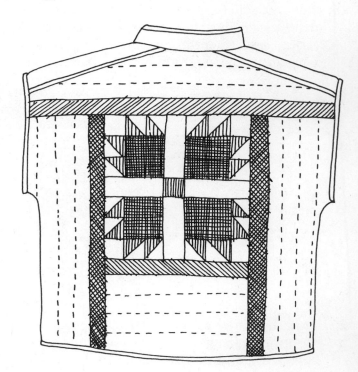

NORA'S RAINBOW VEST

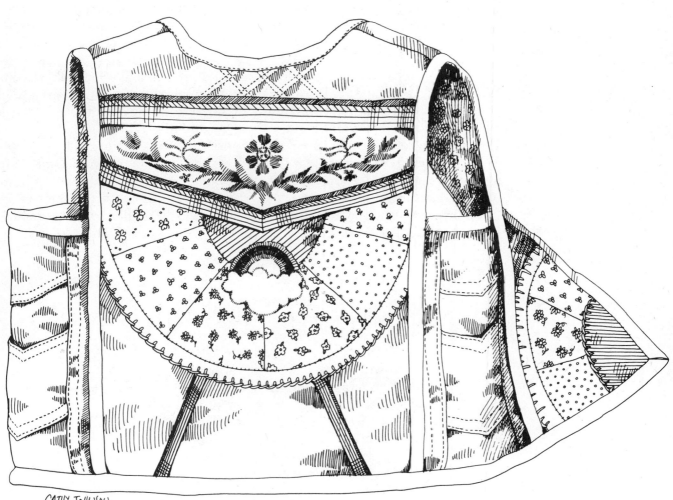

CATHY JOHNSON

This project (see the color section) was made from a pile of old jeans that had outlived their usefulness, leftover bits of bias tape, purchased rainbow-striped grosgrain ribbon and appliqués, and a healthy dose of imagination. Many of today's jeans are highly fanciful, with tucks and corded designs, embroidery, pockets in a myriad of shapes and sizes, braided denim, and more. If you have access to these secondhand wonders, many of the things that made this vest special are yours for the recycling.

Wash all old jeans before you begin and lay your pile out to consider the possibilities. Try to choose varying shades—some jeans will be newer, and some will have faded to a soft, almost sky blue. Use these variations in your design rather than trying to find matching shades. Look for fancy details. I was lucky enough to find an embroidered yoke on a pair of child's jeans and tiny pockets that found their way into the side panels. Such a small vest could not hold both pockets, so the upper one became an echoing chevron shape. A pair of my old jeans, paint-spattered and stained, still had sections of a corded design down the side that added interest to the yoke.

You will not find the *same* details I did, but keep an open mind. If you cannot find any fancy jeans, do not despair. The colors themselves make a beautiful tonal variation, and you can add small details of your own. I had originally planned to string quilt the side panels before I discovered the tiny pockets and made them fit. It is possible, too, to use new denim if you cannot find any old jeans. The yardages given here are appropriate for most children between five and eight years old. You can substitute flannel for the batting, or if you are planning a summer vest, omit the batting. This project is a perfect opportunity for you to use up small pieces of double fold bias tape in rainbow colors.

Materials

- a pile of old, clean jeans *or* ½ yard of denim
- ½ yard of bright calico fabric (for lining)
- ½ yard of batting
- ½ yard of lightweight fabric (for backing)
- ¼ yard of solid fabric (for appliqué)
- fabric scraps in bright colors for Dresden Plate (twelve different colors, or repeat some front and back)
- 20 inches of 1-inch rainbow ribbon
- 9 inches of ¾-inch rainbow ribbon
- 1 yard of narrow (almost ½-inch) rainbow ribbon
- one spool *each* of red and blue thread (blue should be heavy-duty)
- one skein *each* of red and yellow embroidery thead (or your favorite rainbow colors)
- one package *each* of wide bias tape in red, yellow, and green
- one package *each* of double fold bias tape in red and yellow
- two small rainbow appliqués
- one rainbow-and-cloud appliqué

1. This is a simple, make-your-own child's vest pattern, based loosely on a Yvonne Porcella design. Measure your youngster from shoulder to waist or to desired vest length (**A**), around the chest (**B**), across the chest from armhole to armhole (**C**), and from the shoulder to the armhole depth (**D**), as shown in figure 12–1. Add 2 inches for wearing ease to the chest measurement. Write these figures down, as you will draft your pattern from them.

2. Some people measure directly onto the fabric, but I prefer to make a pattern, not only to make the project less nerve-racking, but to have a pattern for future use. Newspaper or tracing paper will work well. Draw two rectangles as shown in figure 12–2, using shoulder-to-waist measurement (**A**) and chest width (**C**) and adding ½ inch for seam allowances all around. Find the center of one rectangle and draw a line lengthwise. Mark 1 inch down on the side seams for fitted shoulders and draw a line from the center to that mark.

Directions

12–1. Measure as shown.

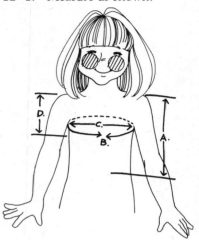

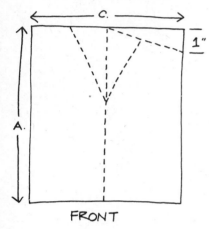

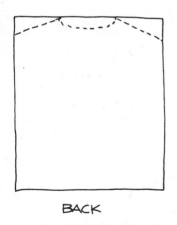

12–2. Cut as shown for pattern.

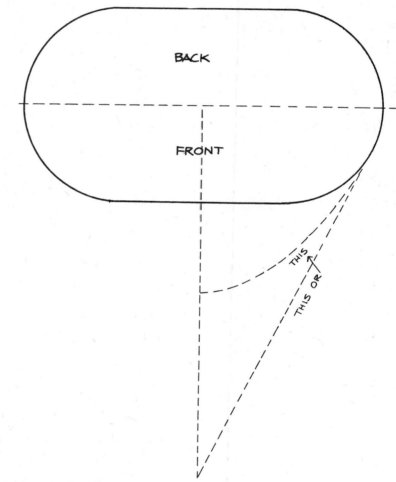

12–3. Neck template.

3. Enlarge the oval neck template provided in figure 12–3, or simply measure the width of the child's neck plus 1 inch. Center oval on top edge of each rectangle, as shown, and transfer the shape. Cut along neck and shoulder lines (see fig. 12–2). Cut one rectangle apart along the center for vest back. Cut vest front along center line and choose the modified V neck or the high,

round-necked opening (see fig. 12–3) for vest front.

4. Subtract the width of both (front and back) rectangles from your child's chest measurement; this will give you the width of the side panels. Remember to include the extra 2 inches for wearing ease. Divide this number in half for the two panels and add another ½ inch at the sides for seam allowances.

5. Find the shoulder to armhole depth from your child's measurements and add 1 inch for wearing ease. Mark on your front and back rectangles. The remaining distance between that mark and the bottom of the vest gives you the depth of the side panels. Cut a paper pattern to these dimensions (fig. 12–4).

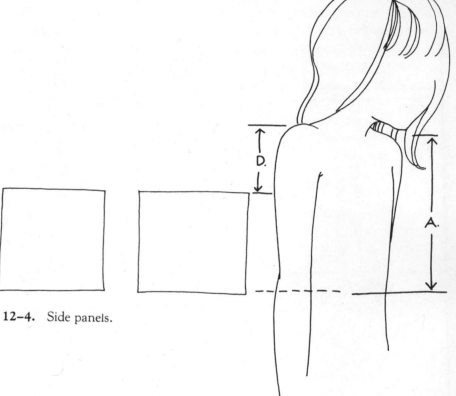

12–5. Plan piecing details.

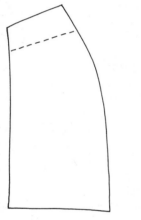

FRONT

12–4. Side panels.

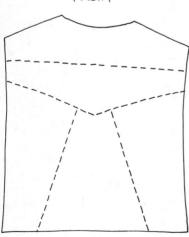

BACK

6. Now cut two *each* of the side panels and fronts from lining, backing, and batting. Cut one vest back pattern from lining, backing, and batting.

7. Use the backing fabric as a piecing guide for the denim. If you are using existing jeans details, their size will determine the exact measurements of such things as yoke depth. You may wish to make an extra paper pattern for vest fronts and back. Draw your piecing design on the extra pattern, then cut it apart to guide you in planning details. Remember to add ½ inch along the new cutting lines for seam allowances or overlap. Figure 12–5 shows the piecing guide for my vest.

8. If using old jeans, cut them along the leg seams and open them out to make flat yardage. When laying out your pattern on the jeans fabric, try to utilize the straight grain of the fabric wherever possible. If a special detail you want to use makes this impossible, do not worry about it. Some rules were made to be broken!

9. To add a central ray of darker denim for interest, fold a piece of

paper and cut a wide diagonal. The length is determined by the size of the vest and the other details.

10. The shape of the flowered yoke from an old pair of jeans determined the chevron-shaped piece on the vest back, but it is easy to cut a similar shape. Just make the point in the center a bit lower than the sides, and the width the same as the vest back.

11. In order to avoid extra bulk, I omitted seam allowances in some areas—yoke bottom, chevron, etc. Denim is a heavy fabric, and I wanted to be sure I could sew through all the layers on my old machine. Where you plan to cover fabric edges with ribbon you can safely cut away the seam allowances and stitch denim down directly to the batting and backing as shown in figure 12-6. Cover all edges with ribbon, but do not sew down the bottom of the chevron at this point.

12. The finished Dresden Plate (or half-plate) should be approximately 1 inch less wide than the width of the back. Either use an existing pattern to fit, or cut and fold a circle of paper the right size for your measurements. Fold the circle in half, then half again, then into thirds. Cut out center if desired, or leave it in to omit center appliqué. Cut the circle apart along fold lines, adding ¼-inch seam allowances along the cutting lines (fig. 12-7). Plan out color positioning and assemble Dresden Plate pieces, sewing six together to form a half-circle and the remaining pieces together in threes to make two quarter-circles.

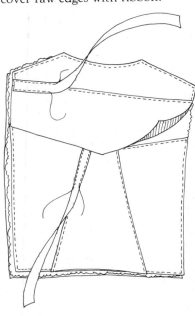

12-6. Sew denim details and cover raw edges with ribbon.

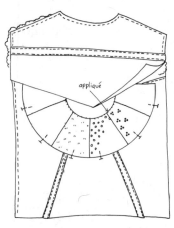

12-8. Appliqué assembled Dresden Plate in place and cover raw edges in the center.

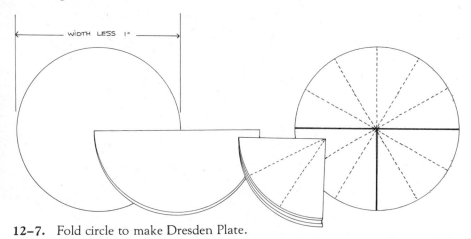

12-7. Fold circle to make Dresden Plate.

13. Position Dresden Plate semicircle so that the upper edge is covered by the chevron. Pin in place. Cut a semicircle of solid fabric to cover the center of the plate and appliqué in place (fig. 12-8).

14. Steam a piece of double fold bias tape to cover the raw edge at the bottom of the plate, curving as you press. Pin. Hand or machine stitch in place.

15. Add a decorative embroidery stitch, such as the simple buttonhole stitch, along the lower edge of the Dresden Plate (fig. 12-9).

16. Sew lower edge of chevron down over the upper edge of the Dresden Plate and cover the raw edges with rainbow ribbon. Make a tuck at the point of the chevron. I added the optional rainbow-and-cloud appliqué at this point (fig. 12-10).

17. On the vest front, large denim pieces cover the entire backing/ batting piece. Edgestitch all around and add yoke pieces as

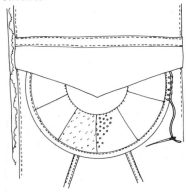

12-9. Cover lower edges with bias tape and add decorative stitches.

NORA'S RAINBOW VEST

12–10. Optional appliqué and ribbon trim.

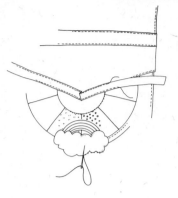

12–11. See steps 17 and 18.

12–12. Add rainbow appliqués.

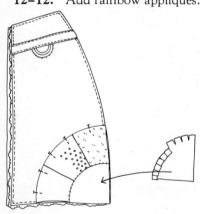

shown. Cover raw edges with rainbow ribbon and stitch top edge of ribbon (fig. 12–11).

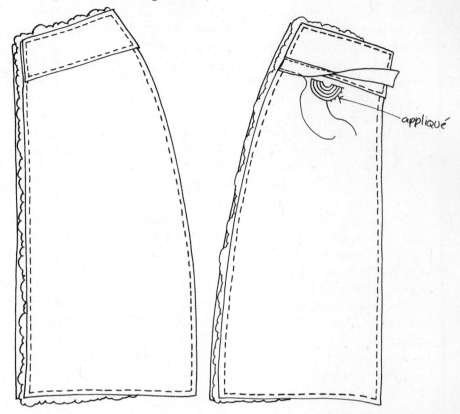

appliqué

18. Pin small rainbow appliqués in place and cover the top edge with the lower edge of the ribbon. Tack down appliqués and ribbon.
19. Position one quarter-circle Dresden Plate on each center front corner and pin in place. Cut quarter-circles for center appliqués. Clip and turn curved edges and appliqué in place (fig. 12–12).
20. Cover outer edges of quarter-circle plates with bias tape, as you did in steps 14 and 15.
21. Assemble side sections. If you are using a bulky detail, such as pockets, omit batting and sew around all edges. Add lining fabric to this "sandwich," right side out. Otherwise, string quilt horizontally on side sections.
22. Bind upper edge *only* of side sections with wide bias tape.
23. Pin lining fabric in place on front and back vest pieces, right side out. Edgestitch if desired.
24. Sew shoulder seams, right sides together. Press open and trim to ¼ inch. Cover inside seams with wide bias tape.
25. Sew side panels to front and back, *wrong sides together*. The seam will be on the outside. Bind with wide bias tape, continuing over the shoulder from waist to waist. Fold the side panels back out of the way so only the seam allowances are caught in the binding. Turn to cover raw edges and stitch by hand, as shown in figure 12–13.
26. Bind remaining edges (neck, front, vest bottom) with wide bias tape. Turn to the inside and hand stitch to lining.
27. Ribbon ties complete the vest. Use either a single narrow ribbon or a cascade of tiny grosgrain ribbons in rainbow colors, knotted at the ends and sewn to the vest front for a festive closure.

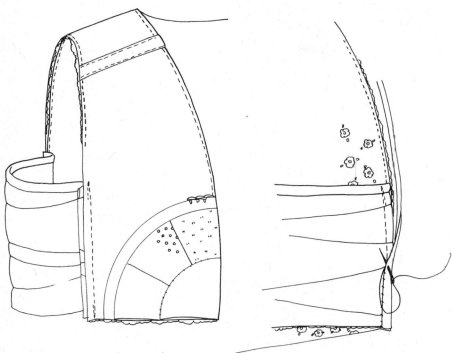

28. As a special finishing touch, you may want to add an appliqué to the lining. I used a bright red heart to contrast with the yellow calico of the lining fabric.

Instead of strong primary colors and rainbows, make your vest with pastels and heavy crocheted lace. A flower appliqué would be pretty in place of rainbows. Secondhand or new doilies could take the place of Dresden Plates for a feminine effect.

A boy's vest could have solid colors and a baseball appliqué. If you want, appliqué a favorite animal on the back panel (figure 12–14).

The Personal Touch

12–14. A fancy vest and a boy's vest.

MOLLY'S DREAM JUMPER

CATHY JOHNSON

This jumper combines all of a young lady's favorites—lavender and lace, flowers, and patchwork. The border of the skirt even features favorite motifs quilted in. You could use your own special kid's favorites, or do all hearts—a few of the patterns are included with this chapter. Coloring books or craft pattern books are good sources for simple designs.

Since the jumper front is narrower than most quilt square designs, I folded and graphed my own pattern. It was designed especially to accommodate the purchased fancywork square in the middle, so the central square is somewhat larger than the others. The pattern is included for the patchwork block, as are the directions for graphing your own to size. Thanks to Jinny Beyer and her folding techniques (see *Sourcebooks*), it is easy to make whatever size you need.

This is the Churn Dash pattern—any simple quilt square will do as well. Since it *is* rather small, it is best to keep the design fairly uncomplicated. Unless you are a *truly* accomplished quilter this is not the best place for a Pine Tree or Goose in the Pond quilt square.

The quilted band on the skirt adds warmth and fullness. No need for a crinoline to hold this skirt out! I adapted the jumper from a commercial pattern with a high waist and an apron-type skirt. I simply lengthened the waist measurement and made the skirt all in one piece, which necessitated a new back opening. And I added 1½ inches to each side of the back to accommodate the Velcro closures.

The fabric yardages are for a size 10 girl's pattern. It is best to use all one fabric for this jumper (all cotton or all polycotton) because different fabrics handle differently and you may get puckers at the seams. When choosing fabrics, think of color variation as well as tone variation. As you will see in the photo in the color section, my basic color was lavender. So I picked blues and pinks to mix with my range of lavenders and violets.

Materials

- ▢ jumper or pinafore pattern
- ▢ fabric A: 2½ yards fabric (for backing and skirt)
- ▢ fabric B: ½ yard lightweight fabric (for lining)
- ▢ quilting fabrics: ¼ yard *each* of six different fabrics
- ▢ ½ yard of calico fabric (for bias binding)
- ▢ 1 yard of lightweight batting
- ▢ 1 yard *each* of two brocaded ribbons
- ▢ 2½ yards of a different ribbon
- ▢ 2½ yards of a matching solid-color ribbon
- ▢ 3 yards of narrow crocheted lace
- ▢ one large spool of thread to match color of jumper
- ▢ one spool of white quilting thread
- ▢ one package of hem facing
- ▢ one package of Velcro dot fasteners
- ▢ one fancy embroidered and lacy square (optional)

Directions

1. Take the following measurements, as shown in figure 13–1: armhole to armhole (**A**), shoulder to waist (**B**), waist to hem (**C**), and

waist (**D**). Measure the shoulder width (**E**) as well, so straps will be wide enough to stay put on childish shoulders. Lay out your pattern and make necessary adjustments. If your pattern lacks a back opening, fold back pattern piece lengthwise and cut along the fold. Add 1½ inches to each side to allow for overlap for buttons, snaps, or other closures. The skirt can simply be cut in one piece to your skirt length plus hem and top seam allowance. Add 4 inches to skirt length.

2. Cut skirt—2½ yards long and as deep as your skirt length plus 4 inches—from fabric A. (Cutting on the lengthwise grain of the fabric eliminates the need for seams except in the back.)

3. Cut out bodice from fabric A, fabric B, and the batting. Pin fabric A and batting together and baste or stabilize with tailor tacks.

4. Measure the front width of your bodice and cut a square from paper using that dimension for the sides. If you have a purchased fancywork square for the center, position it in the middle of the paper square and mark its dimensions on the paper. Extend the lines on all four sides to the edges of the paper (fig. 13–2). Mark the Churn Dash pattern as shown. Cut the pattern apart to make a template; add ¼-inch seam allowance all around. You will need to cut a central square from quilting fabrics.

5. If you have no central square of purchased fancywork to worry about, making the quilt block pattern is easy. Just fold the bodice. Cut square in thirds in both directions as shown (fig. 13–3). Measure corner squares diagonally and mark. Find the center of the remaining outer squares and mark as shown. Cut out paper pattern and add ¼-inch seam allowances. This "fold, mark, and cut" technique can be used for any quilt pattern, from Nine Patch to the more complicated Jacob's Ladder.

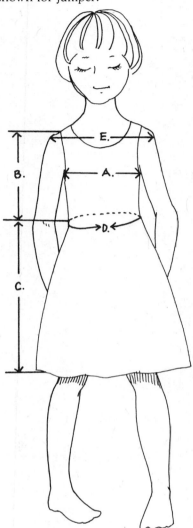

13–1. Take measurements as shown for jumper.

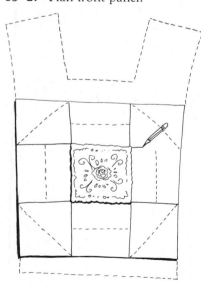

13–2. Plan front panel.

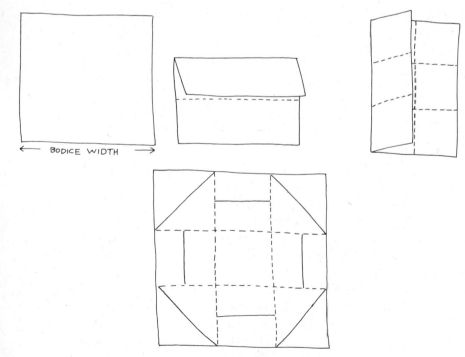

BODICE WIDTH

13–3. Fold paper to make pattern.

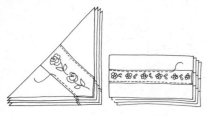

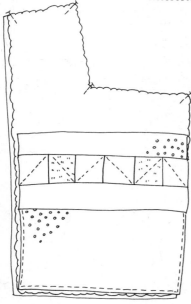

13–5. Add pieced strip for interest.

6. If you plan to add brocade ribbon, sew it in place by machine *before* piecing fabrics, as shown in figure 13–4. Cut quilt square pieces from fabric. Piece together by hand or machine. (Oddly enough, it is easier to piece these by hand.)

7. If you are using a purchased lacy block, position it in place in the center of your block and stitch it down tightly.

8. Center quilt block on jumper front and baste in place. Hand quilt around pieces (see tips in *Beginnings*). If you are *not* using a lace square for the center block, this is a good place to hand quilt a repeat of one of the skirt's motifs.

9. Cut strips from several of your fabrics in various widths, from 1 to 2½ inches.

10. Review the hints on string quilting in *Beginnings*. Add strips till you reach the shoulder seam. Add brocade ribbons or lace by topstitching in place over strips.

11. For back of jumper, cut one wide strip of fabric, about 4 to 5 inches. Stitch in place at bottom of back string and quilt one 2-inch strip to this wide strip.

12. For design interest, piece one strip of 2-inch squares. Sew this in place, then continue adding strips until you reach the back shoulder seam (fig. 13–5). Hand quilt in desired pattern. (Hand quilting is optional here, but it helps to integrate the design with the front block.)

13. Sew one strip of fabric parallel to the shoulder seams and 1½ inches from the seam, as shown, on front and back (fig. 13–6). Turn back and press. Accentuate with ribbon or lace. Trim away excess fabric, using backing as a cutting guide.

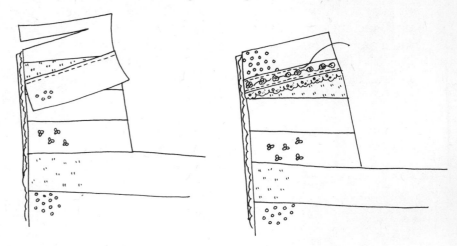

13–6. Finish shoulders as shown, adding lace.

14. Sew shoulder seams. Cut away some of the batting (to reduce bulk) and press seam open.

15. Sew shoulder seams of bodice lining (fabric B) and pin in place, *wrong sides together*, on bodice. Edgestitch to hold the fabric "sandwich" together.

16. See section on seam finishes in *Beginnings*. Cut bias binding 1½ inch wide from calico. Press down ¼ inch along one side.

17. Sew bias binding in place on *right* side of jumper. Stretch binding as you sew on inside corners and fold as shown on outside corners to allow for mitering (fig. 13–7).

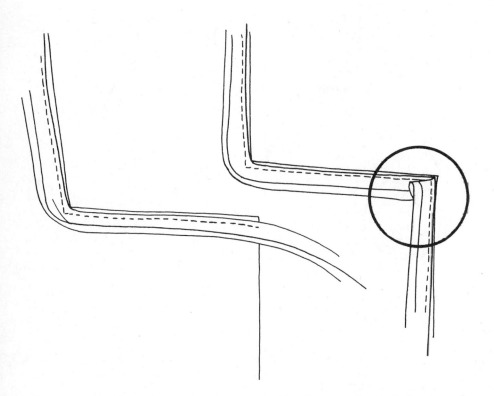

18. Turn folded edge to the inside of bodice and stitch by hand, mitering corners neatly.
19. Mark hem line on skirt by measuring from the waist to skirt length. Mark with tailor's chalk, pencil, or "invisible" marker.
20. Construct a piece of batting 2½ yards (cut from 1-yard piece and lap to make necessary length) by 6 inches and machine baste in place on the *right* side of the skirt, lining up the lower edge with the hem line marked on the skirt (fig. 13–8).

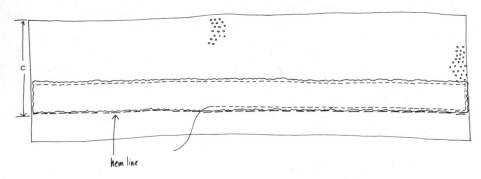

hem line

13–8. Baste batting to *right* side of skirt fabric.

21. Cut strips of fabric 6 inches long and in random widths: some 2 inches, some 3 inches, and some 6 inches. String piece in place the length of the batting strip. Try to vary the colors and widths for greatest interest. You will quilt the wide pieces, so place them at pleasing intervals around the skirt. Topstitch ribbon or lace in place on fabric strips as desired.
22. Trim away excess fabric and batting from top and bottom. Cover raw edges with ribbon. (A less expensive but also less elegant cover-up would be bias tape.)
23. For the skirt's bottom edge, stitch narrow lace to the bottom of the lower ribbon. The lace will extend below the edge when the skirt is hemmed (fig. 13–9).

13–9. Finish pieced strip as shown.

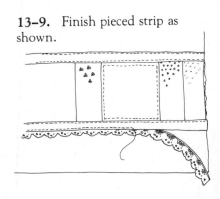

24. Hand quilt designs in the 6-inch squares, using the quilting patterns given in figure 13–10 or patterns of your own.

13–10. Suggested quilting designs for larger pieces.

13–11. Zigzag over heavy thread and pull to gather.

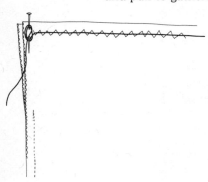

25. Zigzag or turn under the raw edges of the skirt to prevent raveling. Carefully match the edges of the decorative band and pin the skirt at the seam, wrong sides together. Sew, leaving the top 4 inches open for dressing ease. Press seam open.

26. Stitch hem facing in place at the bottom of the skirt. Turn up so the lace is at the lower edge and pin. Hand stitch the hem on the underside.

27. Mark the top edge of the skirt at the center and in quarters with pins or by notching. (Hint: folding and pinning is the easiest way.) To gather skirt, zigzag over heavy buttonhole thread as shown in figure 13–11. Secure one end of the thread and pull the other for a quick gather. Another method is to take two rows of machine basting across the top edge. Pull evenly to gather.

28. Cut two waistbands, each 2¼ inches by the waist measurement plus 3 inches. Trim top of one waistband with ribbon; the top of the ribbon should be ½ inch from the top of the band. Turn ½-inch seam allowance to wrong side of top of both waistbands and press. Pin or notch at centers and quarters of *lower* edge of the waistbands.

29. Distribute skirt gathers evenly. Match marks on skirt and trimmed waistband. Pin, wrong sides together, and sew.

30. Pin the other waistband on the inside of the skirt, right side of band to wrong side of skirt. Using the first line of stitching as a guide, sew waistband in place. Stitch ends up, as shown, with top seam allowance still folded (fig. 13–12). Clip corners and turn waistbands up.

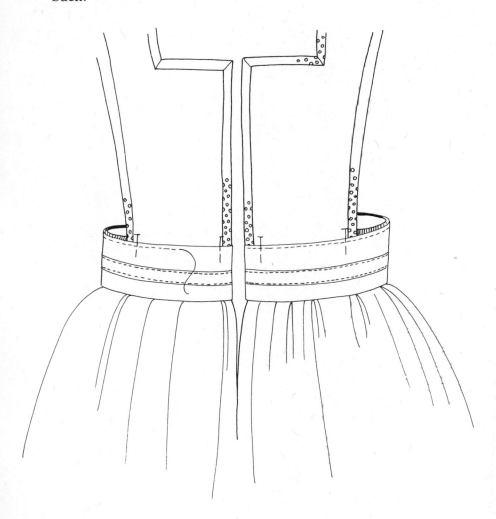

13–12. Add a second waistband piece.

31. Press waistbands, with the top seam allowance still inside. You now have an open "pocket" to receive the jumper bodice. Match the center of the bodice front with the center of the waistband and pin in place (fig. 13–13).
32. Pin the back edges of the bodice in place, lined up with the ends of the waistband. Topstitch through all layers to attach bodice to waistband.
33. Try on and sew waistband hooks and Velcro closures to jumper back.

13–13. Enclose bodice lower edge in waistband and stitch.

The Personal Touch

Try a more traditional interpretation of the quilted skirt—fold up a very deep hem (at least half the skirt length) to enclose a wide band of batting and hand quilt design in place. Another variation is to add ruffles at the shoulders and skirt bottom for a storybook look (fig. 13–14).

A simpler construction method consists of a quilt square front and apron-style straps—then the only closure necessary is on the waistband. You could also make the entire jumper into an apron. Leave the skirt back open and tie the waist with long streamers.

Sheer fabric appliqués add a charming touch. Try several sheer white fabrics—dotted swiss, organdy, voile. Embellish with embroidery.

13–14. Pretty jumper ideas.

CRAZY QUILT VICTORIAN VEST

Cathy Johnson

This vest is a Victorian crazy quilt adapted for wearing. This particular vest reflects my own love for Victorian design, pattern, decoration, and imaginative use of saved and sentimental things. The patterned velvet is from an antique chaise longue. The solid gold velvet is from a very short minidress that has hidden in my attic since the sixties, along with the black satin fabric bought at a store long out of business. Red taffeta plaid was to have been a Christmas dress, a dress that never happened, and the laces were from my collection gleaned over the years from junk stores and garage sales. The only thing I bought specially for this project (see the color section) was the brocade ribbon—and it was the catalyst that brought it all together.

A similar creation could, of course, be made from all new fabrics, ribbons, and laces. But look around first and see what you can collect to use on your own vest. An old hanky, edged with wonderful lace; threadbare pillowcases whose edges still sport some lovely tatting; a bit from a favorite, sentimental dress, no longer worn; an embroidered monogram from an old silk blouse; antique buttons or beads. These are the raw materials of your own crazy quilt vest. Use your imagination!

The Victorians often signed their creations when finished. Following that tradition, my own initials and the date appear in the lining of this vest. Who knows? Maybe it will be a keepsake someday.

Traditional crazy quilts use no batting, but I wanted my vest to have a soft, puffy look—I also wanted it to be warm! You can omit the batting if you wish. It is difficult to estimate yardages for scraps. Just be sure you have a good variety of scraps on hand so you can place patterns and colors in such a way that the same fabrics will not be next to each other too often. Choose rich, dark colors or depart from the traditional and work with pastels. Silks and satins are especially lovely in a crazy quilt, but wools and corduroys might make an interesting change.

You will also need a pattern for a vest without darts. The darts would add too much bulk. And since there will be so much surface decoration, a vest with a simple cut is best.

Materials

- simple vest pattern
- quilting fabrics: scraps *or* ¼ yard *each* of five different fabrics
- 1 yard of soft muslin (for backing)
- 1 yard of solid fabric (for lining)
- 1 yard of batting
- old lace, doilies, and ribbons *or* 1 yard *each* of varying widths of new lace
- 1 yard *each* of three widths of brocade ribbon
- 1 yard *each* of two or three narrow (¼-inch) satin or grosgrain ribbons
- three skeins of embroidery thread to match or complement your colors
- one spool of thread to match lining fabric
- one spool of thread to match color of lace

1. Make any necessary adjustments in the paper pattern for size. Lengthen or shorten as needed. Now is the time to alter the design if you wish. My pattern already had points in the front—if yours does not and you want them, cut the paper pattern to the desired shape (fig. 14-1).

2. Cut backing, lining, and batting from the adjusted pattern. Pin the batting and the backing fabric together. Baste or secure with tailor tacks and remove pins.

3. Pin side and shoulder seams of the batting/backing to give you an idea of the bulk and fit at the same time. Try it on and make any necessary changes. A lot of work goes into this vest, and believe me, you will want to be able to wear it comfortably!

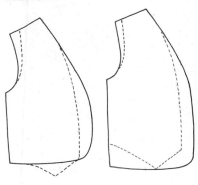

14-1. Change your pattern as desired.

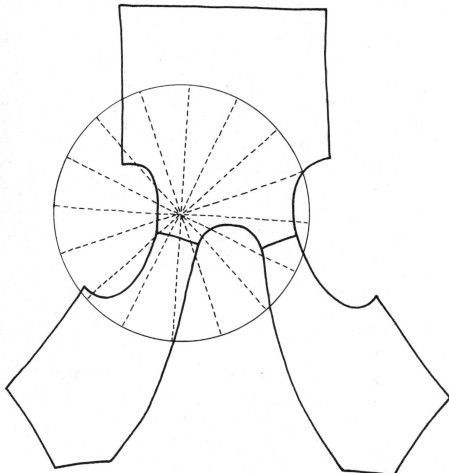

14-2. Asymmetrical Dresden Plate placement.

4. For design definition and interest, I wanted an asymmetrical yoke area using the Dresden Plate pattern. To get the size right, sew the shoulder seams of the batting/backing pieces and open the vest out flat as shown in figure 14-2. The circle needs to be larger, so measure the diameter needed to cover the yoke area (shown) and draw a circle on paper to that size. Cut out the circle, fold it in half and half again, until it is divided into sixteen wedges. Cut out one wedge to use as a pattern, adding ¼-inch seam allowances to the sides of the wedge.

5. Cut sixteen wedges from your fabrics.

6. Topstitch bits of ribbon or lace to some of the wedges as desired —lengthwise, horizontally, or diagonally.

7. Sew the wedges together in fours to form quarter-circles, then

14–3. Dresden Plate with one seam left unsewn.

together again to make half-circles. This will ensure the pieces fit together smoothly. Sew one side of the circle to the other, leaving one side open as shown in figure 14–3.

8. Lay the batting/backing pieces down on the Dresden Plate. Experiment with placement, then pin backing all around the edges of the circle as well as the vest edges as shown in figure 14–4. Use the backing piece as a guide and cut away the parts of the circle that extend beyond the vest itself. *Save these pieces* to use in the vest body.

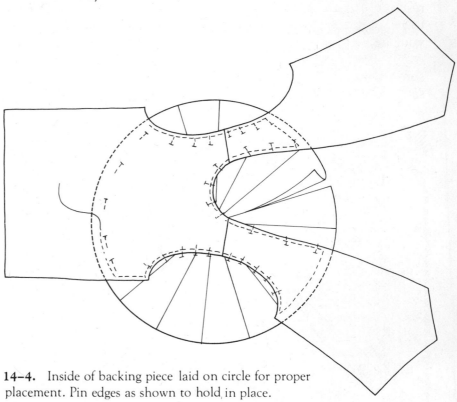

14–4. Inside of backing piece laid on circle for proper placement. Pin edges as shown to hold in place.

14–5. Crazy quilting.

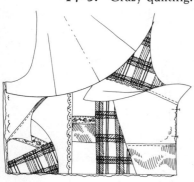

14–6. Finishing your crazy-quilted design.

9. Baste the circle in place around the neck and armholes, stopping 1 inch before the outer edge of the circle. Baste in 1 inch from the curved edge all around. (This will allow you to slip the raw edges of the quilt pieces under the circle.)

10. The rest of the vest is true crazy quilting. Using string quilting techniques (see the tips in *Beginnings*), cover as many raw edges as you can by machine. Remember to add ribbon or lace as you sew—it can be used to hide raw edges as well as to enhance the Victorian effect. Since you cut these pieces in random shapes, you will not be able to hide all the seams as you do in straight string piecing. Some will have to be turned and stitched by hand, using blindstitch or appliqué stitch (fig. 14–5). Remember when assembling a crazy quilt to plan ahead. Create as you go, yes; but plan what pieces go on first, which embellishments can be added by machine, and how best to hide raw edges.

11. Continue adding random-shaped pieces until the entire vest body is covered and all raw edges are hidden. Small pieces of fabric in interesting shapes can be appliquéd on to cover raw edges if necessary (fig. 14–6). Crazy quilting should extend under the edge and to the basting line of the Dresden Plate.

12. Turn under the edge of the Dresden Plate all around and blind-stitch or appliqué firmly in place (fig. 14–7). Turn vest face down and trim away excess fabric, using backing as a cutting guide.

13. If you enjoy embroidery and wish to make a really authentic-looking crazy quilt, decorate any or all edges. The vest becomes a kind of sampler of embroidery stitches, as did the original crazy quilts. Accentuate Dresden Plate wedges with chain stitches, feather stitch, sheaf of wheat, or variations. Lace together parallel rows of ribbon with a simple herringbone stitch. The rest of the vest may be decorated in the same fashion. Remember to use contrasting embroidery thread on adjoining fabrics so your handiwork will show.

   See the sampler of embroidery stitches in figure 14–8 for some ideas to get you started, and embroider until you are satisfied with the result.

14–7. Stitch down edge of Plate, then trim with lace.

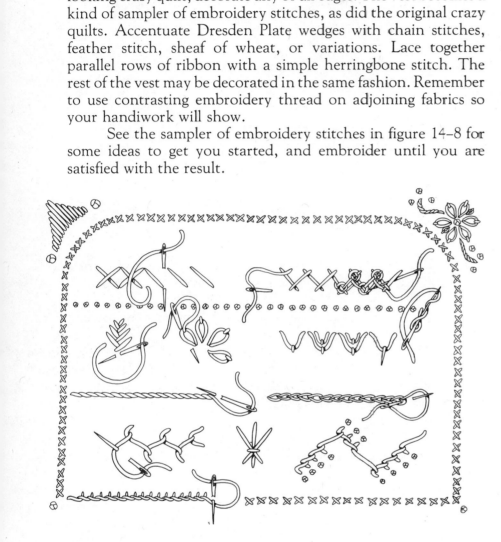

14–8. Embroidery Stitch Sampler.

14. If desired, embroider your initials or other details on the lining fabric now. Sew shoulder seams of lining fabric, right sides together. Press open.

15. Pin lining to vest, right sides together. Sew bottom, armholes, front, and neck as shown in figure 14–9, leaving side seams open. Trim seams and clip curves and points as necessary.

16. Reach into vest through the back side seam and grasp the inside of one vest front. (You may need to start the turning process from the front since the shoulders are too narrow for most hands to reach through.) Keep pulling out all fabric still inside through the same open seam until the entire vest is right side out (fig. 14–10).

17. Sew side seams of vest fabric by machine, pulling lining back out of the way. Extend seam an inch or two into the lining fabric if possible. Trim or grade seam allowances if necessary, and carefully press seam open. A pressing ham is a help here.

18. Stitch lining shut by hand to finish vest.

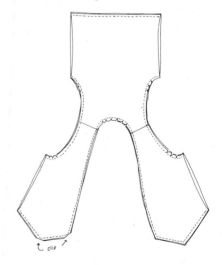

14–9. See step 15.

14-10. Clip and turn vest and lining as one.

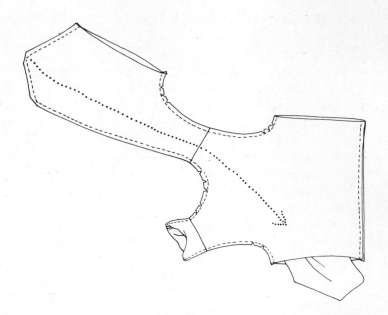

The Personal Touch

Consider using only one color but different fabrics—for instance, velvet, moiré silk, taffeta, and printed velveteen, all in shades of maroon.

Make a crazy quilt vest using old ties with rich, understated patterns.

If you have access to old silk lingerie with beautiful lace trim, make a vest from white, off-white, cream, and flesh colors. Make use of interesting shapes formed by slip hems and necklines. A knockout for evening—try pearl beads sewn on at random or in patterns to add to the elegant feeling (fig. 14-11).

If a vest is not to your taste or seems like too much work, try a crazy-quilted yoke on a caftan or dress. A child's jumper of velveteen or corduroy could be wonderful with a crazy quilt bodice.

14-11. Crazy quilting with lingerie and as a dress bodice.

SEMINOLE SHIRT

CATHY JOHNSON

Decoration, rather than warmth, is the issue here, although the myriad seam allowances of Seminole work do make for air spaces that hold in body heat. A thin layer of cotton flannel acts as padding for optional lightweight quilting.

You can get as elaborate as you like with Seminole work. This project is only moderately difficult but is somewhat complicated by use of a wide range of fabrics. Soft, supple plaid blends, stiffer kettle-cloth, cotton calico—these gave me beautiful colors to work with, but it would have made for an easier project to stitch (and to press) had I used all one weight and fabric content. Pressing the seam allowances of such varied fabrics requires the patience of Job!

If your shirt pattern has a separate yoke piece, you will want to pin it and the shirt body together to form the smooth lining of the Seminole work yoke. You can use the yoke pattern as a guide for the shape of the finished yoke. Also, the pattern should have a separate (not self-facing) front-button placket. The yardages that follow are for a man's size medium. Pick lightweight fabrics: cottons, polycottons, or the new, very lightweight corduroy.

Materials

- man's shirt pattern
- 3⅛ yards of solid fabric (for shirt)
- ¼ yard *each* of five or more solid fabrics, at least 45 inches wide (for Seminole work)
- ¼ yard of calico or stripe fabric (optional)
- ½ yard of lightweight flannel or batting (optional)
- 1⅛ yards of fusible interfacing
- two spools of thread to match color of shirt fabric
- two packages of gripper snaps

Directions

1. Make any necessary adjustments on the paper pattern—lengthen or shorten sleeves, shirttail, etc. If your pattern has a separate yoke, pin the yoke piece to the main pattern piece to provide a smooth backing for the Seminole work section. All those seam allowances need protection in the wash.
2. Cut out main pattern pieces from the shirt fabric. If you want to add an interesting contrast, cut the undercollar and one collar band from calico. You can also cut the wrong side of the placket from calico. Cut *four* cuffs, two will form the stabilizing backs for the Seminole work.
3. Review the section on Seminole work in *Beginnings*. Cut strips for Seminole work, some 1½ inches wide, some 1 inch, and some ¾ inch. Plan ahead for contrast. Cut some strips from the shirt fabric; this will help integrate the patchwork panels with the shirt. Remember to keep all strips the same length for ease in piecing and cutting.
4. Sew two, three, or four strips together lengthwise as shown, taking a ¼-inch seam and varying color or value for good contrast (fig. 15–1).

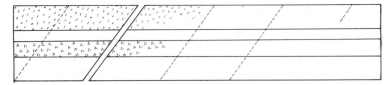

15-1. Sew long strips together.

5. If you are sewing narrow ¾-inch strips, which tend to become inaccurate, wavy lines if sewn normally with fabric to the left of the presser foot and seam allowances to the right, try this: sew the first seam allowance in the normal manner, as shown in figure 15–2. Then sew the second seam using the first line of stitches as a sewing guide instead of the cut edges of the fabric strips, as in the illustration. Keep the *left* edge of your presser foot lined up with the first seam line to produce a uniform line.

6. Press all seam allowances down carefully, trying not to stretch or distort the band.

7. My Seminole work designs for this shirt are simple and fairly uniform. All cuts along the length of the bands are made 1½ inches apart. Mark and cut carefully, as shown in figure 15–3, the length of the band.

15-3. Cut at 1½-inch intervals.

8. Sew these pieces together with an offset as shown in figure 15–4. To save time and thread, sew them in twos first, in a long string as shown. Then clip and sew pairs into fours, retaining the same offset. Join the entire band. Press seam allowances to one side.

    Optional: Making diagonal cuts on the lengthwise band produces a different effect (fig. 15–5). It is, however, a bit more confusing and, because of the bias cut, a bit more difficult to work with. Experiment with a few pieces cut this way to see if the finished effect is worth the extra bother to you.

15-5. Make diagonal cuts for a different effect.

9. For a dividing band, choose a ¾-inch strip in a new color or a color you have already used in piecing. Place a dividing band lengthwise on the patchwork band. The easiest method is to line up, right sides together, the edge of the divider band with the innermost points of the band. Sew, taking a ¼-inch seam (fig. 15–6). If you want to be more precise, mark a seam line on the band with tailor's chalk or a pencil and line up the divider band with this mark. Trim down the excess seam from the pieced band to match the edge of the dividing band. Then sew this to

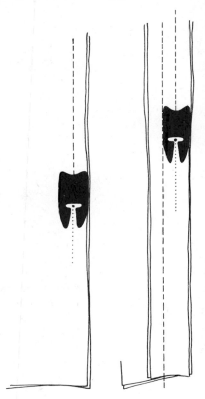

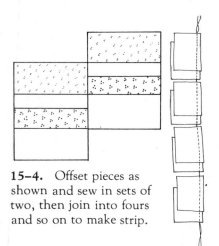

15-4. Offset pieces as shown and sew in sets of two, then join into fours and so on to make strip.

15–6. Line up divider bands along inside edges and stitch.

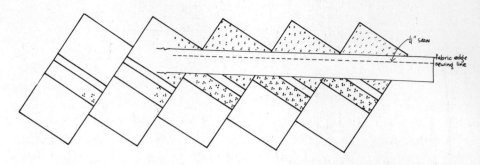

another pieced band, matching dividing band as before. Continue piecing bands and dividers until you have a piece large enough to cover your yoke area. If you like, add stacks of two or three dividing bands as you piece. Remember the tip mentioned in *Beginnings* for sewing ¾-inch bands. It works here, too.

10. I wanted a pointed, Western-style yoke on the shirt back, but I did not want the Seminole bands to continue down to the point. I chose to add solid strips of varying widths (fig. 15–7). Using your yoke pattern, cut the Seminole piece to shape. Turn bottom edge under ¼ inch and press.

15–7. Complete yoke point as shown.

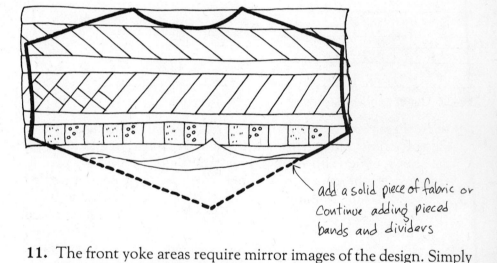

add a solid piece of fabric or continue adding pieced bands and dividers

11. The front yoke areas require mirror images of the design. Simply construct half of the Seminole band with the offset in one direction, the other band with the offset in the opposite direction. For diagonally cut pieces it is necessary to reverse the angle of the cut as shown in figure 15–8.

15–8. Front bands should be mirror images of each other.

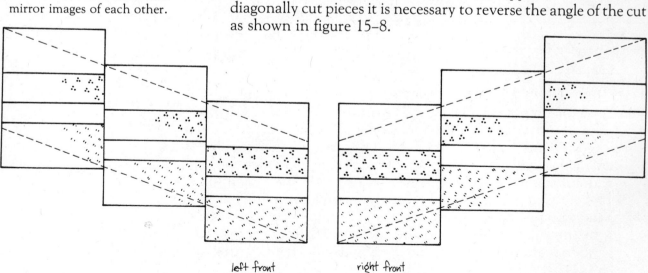

left front   right front

12. Line up the front Seminole pieces to match design and pin patterns down (fig. 15–9). Transfer pattern shape with tailor's chalk and remove patterns. Fold back along center lines and double-check design match. Make any adjustments. Cut yoke shapes. Turn bottom edges under ¼ inch and press.

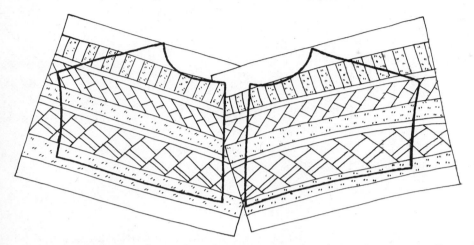

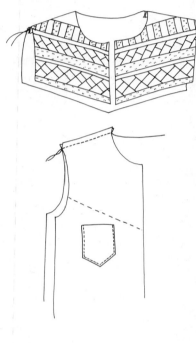

15–9. Trim away excess Seminole work.

15–10. Enclose shoulder seams as shown.

13. *Optional:* Cut flannel or batting to yoke shape *less* seam allowance and baste in place on shirt pieces.

14. For a clean, finished effect, you will want to cover or enclose as many of the raw edges of the Seminole work as possible. The bands need to be protected in the wash to prevent raveling. Sew shirt shoulder seams together, *wrong* sides together as shown in figure 15–10. Press seam open. Sew Seminole yokes at the shoulders, *right* sides together. Press seams open.

15. Pin yoke in place on shirt body, matching shoulder seams. Topstitch lower edges in place. Machine baste along neck and center front (fig. 15–11). Hand quilt divider strips if desired. This helps stabilize the Seminole work and adds a nice touch—even if you have not used batting.

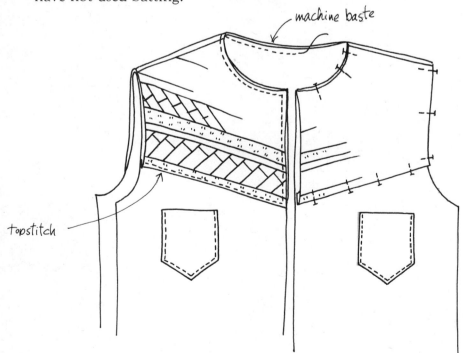

machine baste

topstitch

15–11. Machine stitch and topstitch as shown.

16. Add shirt pockets, following pattern directions.
17. Assemble front placket according to pattern directions and sew in place. Press.
18. Bind sleeve plackets as shown in pattern directions.
19. Sew sleeves to shirt, but press seam allowances *away* from the shirt body to reduce bulk. Zigzag along seam edge to keep the patchwork from raveling. A second line of stitches close to the edge will work if you do not have a zigzag—or overcast by hand.
20. Assemble Seminole bands to fit shirt cuffs. Cut away excess Seminole work if necessary. Machine baste to the *right* side of the upper band.
21. Complete cuff and attach to sleeve according to pattern directions. Edgestitch the cuffs.
22. Hem shirt according to pattern directions.
23. Mark closures and finish shirt.

The Personal Touch

If Seminole patchwork seems like too much work, make string-quilted yardage for yokes and cuffs. The effect is still a knockout. Front band and pocket flaps can be string quilted as well. Machine embroidered designs make a good yoke decoration on a Western-style shirt. President Reagan owns one!

The yoke could be a big Dresden Plate, topstitched in place and quilted. Or for a subtle, elegant look, a quilted yoke in the same fabric is a possibility (fig. 15–12).

15–12. Some further shirt ideas.

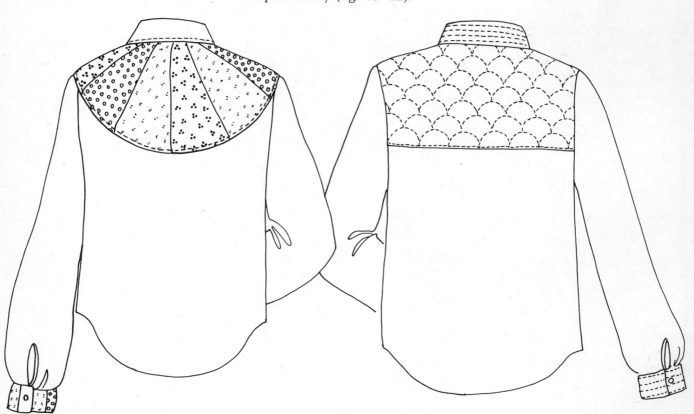

RACHEL'S MACHINE-APPLIQUÉD VEST

CATHY JOHNSON

This vest was designed by Roberta Hammer. Mother, seamstress, dollmaker, artist, and craftswoman, Roberta knows what pleases kids. Machine appliqué is only one of her areas of expertise.

As you can see in the photo (see color section), a collection of bright corduroys—some printed with flowers or plaids, some rich solids—go to make up this vest. Colorful embroidered braid sports tiny ladybugs, and a big tulip with heart-shaped stamens decorates the central medallion. The hand quilted accents worked with cotton crochet thread lend an aura of folkwear.

The vest is a triumph of recycling. The plaid corduroy used as lining was once a man's shirt; the tulip petals were left over from Mama's winter skirt; the flowered fabric came from an erstwhile cozy pillow. The stores are full of beautiful, new printed corduroys, but the challenge of creating a one-of-a-kind garment, a real original, is half the fun. Other fabrics could be used. Sturdy cottons, ginghams, even suedecloth would be satisfying to work with and, with a lightweight batting, warm to wear.

The pattern was from Patch Press. The child's vest is all one piece, making it easier to design front and back as one unit. Any pattern can be pinned together at the side seams to get a similar result. The yardages that follow are for a vest in a child's size 4 to 6.

Materials

- ½ yard of fabric (for lining)
- ⅜ yard of fabric
- ¼ yard *each* of five or six other fabrics *or* scraps from other projects
- ½ yard of bonded quilt batting
- ¼ yard of stabilizing material (permanent pattern maker) to use behind appliqué—newspaper may be substituted
- ⅝ yard of embroidered braid or ribbon
- 1 yard of narrow grosgrain ribbon
- one spool of thread to match body fabric
- one spool of thread to match color of *each* appliqué fabric
- one package of wide bias tape to complement the colors
- two red heart-shaped buttons
- cotton crochet thread
- glue stick

Directions

1. Overlap and pin side seams of your pattern if back is separate from front pieces.
2. Using this adjusted pattern, cut batting. You will appliqué directly on the batting.
3. Plan the appliqué for the central patch or trace and cut out the design provided (fig. 16–1). Cut fabric pieces directly from the pattern; it is not necessary to add seam allowances as you do for hand appliqué.

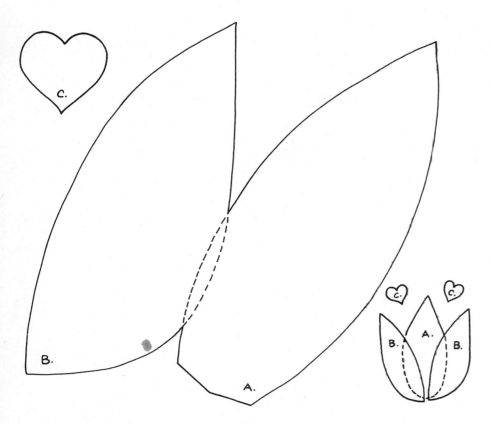

16–2. Hold in place with narrow zigzag, then satin stitch to finish.

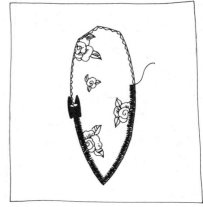

16–3. Stretch fabric to prevent "tunneling."

4. Always start appliqué with the back or bottom piece. Use a glue stick to hold edges in place. Stabilize appliqué with a narrow, open zigzag basting around the edges. (It will not be necessary to do more than the basting stitch in areas that will be covered by subsequent layers of fabric.) Go over the first line of stitching with a wide, tight zigzag (fig. 16–2). You may want to practice a bit on scrap fabrics. If fabric pleats or "tunnels" under zigzag, hold fabric as shown in figure 16–3 as you feed it under the presser foot, stretching it a bit as you sew. If fabric is floppy and warps or puckers around the stitching, use a sheet of stabilizer (permanent pattern maker, for example) under the base fabric (next to the machine's soleplate). When appliqué is finished, trim away stabilizer close to appliqué stitches on the back side. Newspaper may be substituted for background stabilizer—just tear paper away from the back when you are through. Note, however, that newspaper does tend to dull needles quickly.

5. Continue adding fabric pieces until appliqué is finished. Remember to change thread color to match appliqué fabric for best results. However, using black thread for the zigzag satin stitch gives a stained-glass effect.

6. Pin the completed appliqué block in place on the vest back.

7. Piece small blocks to form border design. For fabric that is likely to ravel, such as corduroy, sew blocks together with two close rows of tight stitches, ten to the inch. Appliqué a small heart on one or more of the blocks.

8. Pin rows of blocks in place, making sure that the front blocks line up when the vest is closed, as shown in figure 16–4.

16–4. Position small blocks as shown.

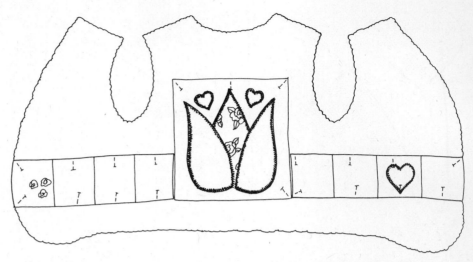

16–5. Cover bottom of large block and finger press seam.

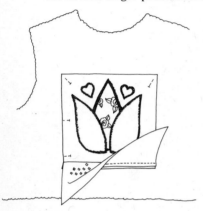

9. Review section on string quilting in *Beginnings*. Cut bottom section the same width as the appliqué block. Lay face down on the edge of the block, stitch, turn and finger press the seam (fig. 16–5). If you are using a napped fabric such as corduroy, finger pressing will avoid flattening the nap. Pressing as you go is a hard habit to break, but finger pressing preserves the puffy look whenever you use string quilting techniques. Pin fabric in place and trim away excess fabric, using batting as a cutting guide.

10. In the same fashion, sew a piece of fabric to cover the top edge of the central block. Turn up, finger press the seam, pin at the neck, and trim the excess fabric.

11. Pin fabric pieces over the upper edge of the front blocks as shown in figure 16–6. Stitch in place, turn up, and finger press. Pin into position and trim fabric away around vest front, shoulders, and armholes.

16–7. Zigzag seams and cover with decorative braid.

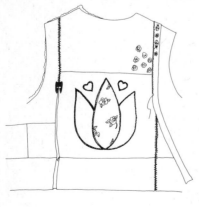

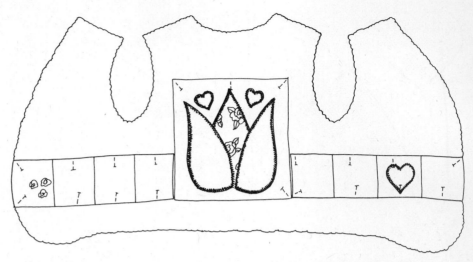

16–6. Finish vest fronts as shown.

12. Pin narrow fabric strips over the bottom of the line of blocks in the same way.

13. You will have raw edges where the central block and the body fabric meet. If you need to, push the edges together and catch in

a wide zigzag—the excess batting will be taken up in the zigzag. Then cover the zigzagged edges with a pretty embroidered braid or ribbon. Use rows of narrow zigzag stitches to hold braid in place, or edgestitch carefully (fig. 16–7).

14. Cut lining fabric, using vest as a cutting guide.
15. Pin shoulder seams of vest, right sides together. To reduce bulk, you may wish to hold *front* batting out of the way while you sew the shoulder seam. (You will not be able to hold back batting out of the way since it will have been caught in the zigzag stitches.) Trim front batting just to seam line (fig. 16–8). Press seam open.
16. Pin the lining shoulder seams, right sides together, and stitch. Press open the seam.
17. Pin vest lining and outside together, matching shoulder seams. Edgestitch to hold in place, if desired.
18. Bind edges with wide bias tape, purchased or made. Finish by hand on the inside. (See tips in *Beginnings*.)
19. Do a line of hand quilting, using a bright crochet thread in a contrasting color, ¼ inch from the edge of the binding. Accent appliqué pieces with hand quilting, if desired.
20. For ties, cut one yard of narrow grosgrain ribbon in half. Make a knot in one end and stitch it to the vest front. Thread a heart-shaped red button onto the ribbon and tie a knot to hold it in place.

Try a vest in shades of pastel gingham. Use different-sized checks for more interest. You might want to use eyelet lace as accents under the edge of braid trim for a little girl's vest.

String quilt the back of the vest above and below the central medallion. Use a favorite motif for the center square, then do a simple Log Cabin design (fig. 16–9). You could also hand quilt a central square—quilt border squares, too!

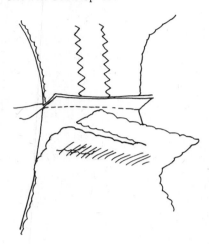

16–8. Finish shoulders as shown. See step 15.

The Personal Touch

16–9. A pretty girl's vest.

WARM, PADDED VEST WITH SEMINOLE TRIM

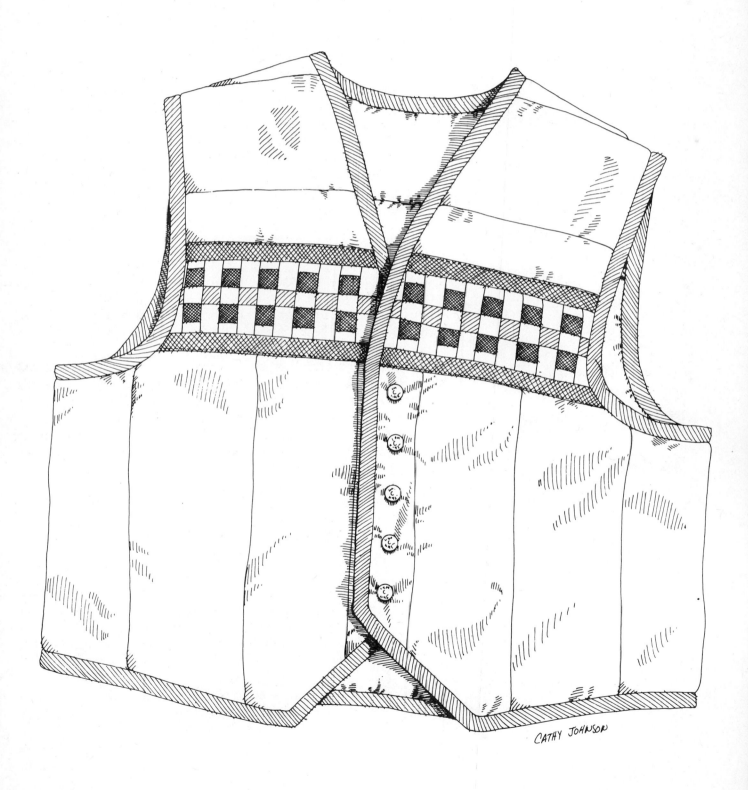

CATHY JOHNSON

Except for its bands of Seminole trim, this vest is simplicity itself—a good, quick project. The channel-quilted fabric (polyester poplin lined with taffeta) is readily available, but you can substitute a vest kit that uses Quallofil or down.

I chose one of the easier Seminole work designs for this trim. Only a bit of advance planning for color placement and a steady hand at the sewing machine are necessary here. The snaps provide an easy closure for winter warmth; omit them for an open vest.

As you will see in the photo (see color section), the design is pattern enough for this vest. I think it's best to avoid prints and stripes and to choose cottons or polycottons in solid colors of harmonizing shades. To avoid extra bulk, pick a pattern without darts and fancy detailing. The yardages that follow are for a man's size medium.

Materials

- □ man's simple vest pattern
- □ 1⅛ yards of channel-quilted polyfil fabric
- □ ¼ yard *each* of four different fabrics (for Seminole bands)
- □ two packages of wide bias tape in a matching color
- □ one spool of thread to match color of channel-quilted fabric
- □ one package of decorative gripper snaps

Directions

1. Lay out your paper pattern and plan any changes. This vest has quilting going horizontally on the yoke and vertically on the body for design interest, so I cut apart my pattern pieces (where the yoke was to be on front and back) and added ½-inch seam allowance to cut edges.

2. Cut fabric from pattern pieces, remembering any directional changes in channel quilting. Cut carefully so quilting lines will match at front edges. In using plump quilted fabric, especially that with a taffeta backing, you may find that the layers will "crawl" a bit at the edges when you cut. To prevent this, make sure your pattern is well pinned through *all* layers of fabric at regular intervals.

3. Sew yokes to front and back pieces with *wrong* sides together. Trim seams to remove excess batting and press open.

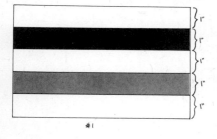

17-1. Seminole strip diagram.

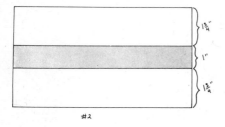

4. Cut Seminole strips as shown in figure 17–1. Band #1 will have all the strips cut in 1-inch widths. Band #2 will have a center strip 1 inch and two outer strips each 1¾ inches wide. Cut strips as long as your fabric is wide, from selvage to selvage. Band #1 has three light strips and two darker colors. Band #2 has two light strips around an intermediate shade.

5. Review the tips on Seminole work in *Beginnings*. Sew strips together along their lengthwise measurement, using ¼-inch seams. Try not to stretch the fabric strips as you sew as that produces a distortion. Press seams down.

6. Measure and cut strips apart at 1-inch intervals. Alternate designs and sew together as shown in figure 17–2. Press all seams to one side.

7. Cut two more 1-inch strips, one from each of your darker colors. Enclose the upper and lower edges of your patchwork bands. Fold back raw edges ¼ inch and press as shown in figure 17–3.

17–2. Cut strips at 1-inch intervals.

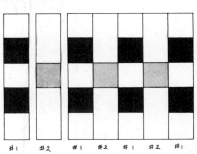

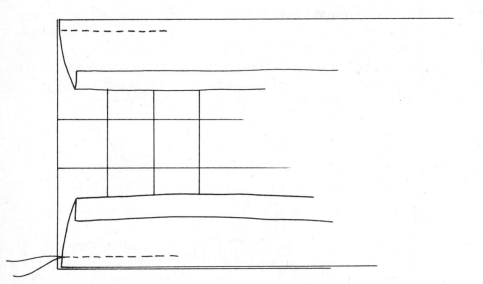

17–3. Enclose edges.

8. On *right* side of vest, position Seminole bands over seams. Make sure bands are aligned to meet in the front. Pin, then edgestitch in place (fig. 17–4).

17–4. Stitch over yoke seam.

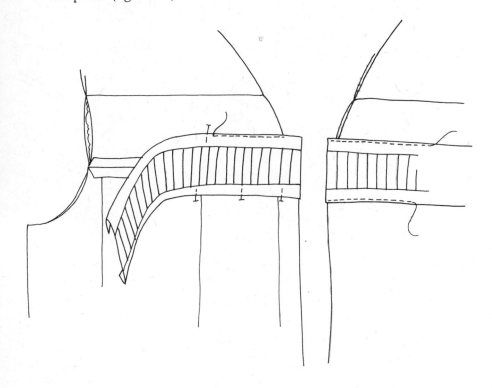

9. Sew shoulder and side seams, right sides together. Trim away excess batting and press seams. Then bind seams with bias tape.
10. Bind all remaining raw edges with wide bias tape. Hand finish on the inside of the vest.
11. Mark and attach gripper snaps according to manufacturer's directions.

WARM, PADDED VEST WITH SEMINOLE TRIM

The Personal Touch

Instead of using the channel-quilted fabric for the yoke, extend Seminole work to the shoulder line with varying bands. Mexican conchos and ties also make an interesting closure. Use leather or fabric ties (fig. 17–5).

For the simplest possible vest, omit the Seminole bands and cover raw edges where the yoke meets the body with wide bias tape.

If you use a down-filled vest kit, follow manufacturer's directions for vest construction and add Seminole bands to personalize the kit. Down "travels" or works its way through many fabrics, so a special fabric is required for the outer shell. Kits include this.

17–5. Two man's vests.

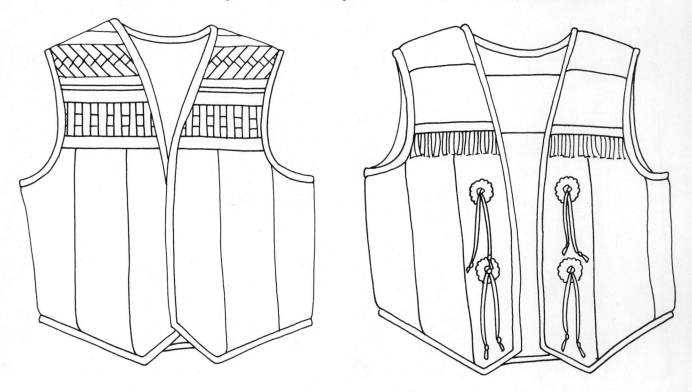

VELVET EVENING VEST

CATHY JOHNSON

A concert in town, dinner at an intimate French restaurant, a gala party, or just a quiet evening by the fire—any of these would be the perfect place to wear this rose-appliquéd evening vest. As you can see in the photograph in the color section, it is an elegant garment.

The vest is deceptively simple. Commercially quilted velvet is used for the body of the vest, and standard—though elegant—string quilting decorates the side panels. The art nouveau roses are made from folded ribbon and fabric. A bit of subtle drama is added by the delicate feather stitches in metallic gold thread.

Moiré lines this particular vest and forms the binding for the edges. You may want to opt for silk, satin, or taffeta.

You cut your own pattern for this vest to your own body measurements, as you would for the *Rainbow Vest*. You might want to make a muslin mock-up first to check the fit. The directions are based loosely on Yvonne Porcella's cutting guide, with changes in the finished vest shape. The yardages are for a woman's size medium.

Materials

- paper (to graph pattern on)
- 1 yard of commercially quilted velvet
- 2¼ yards of moiré (for lining and bias binding)
- small scraps of velvet, crushed velvet, and velour *or* ¼ yard *each* of four or five different fabrics (for side panels)
- ¼ yard of bonded quilt batting
- 1 yard *each* of several shades of satin ribbon in wide and medium widths (for roses)
- 1 yard of velvet cording in a contrasting color (for ties and rose stem)
- small scraps of green velvet and silk (for leaves)
- one spool of metallic gold thread
- one package of pearl "wheat" beads
- one spool of thread to match *each* of the colors you use for the rose and leaves
- several shades of embroidery floss (greens, mauves, pinks)

Directions

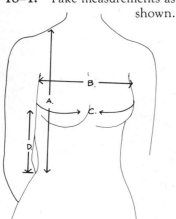

18–1. Take measurements as shown.

1. Take your measurements as shown in figure 18–1: waist (or desired length) to shoulder (**A**), chest (**B**), bust (**C**), and shoulder to armhole depth (**D**). Decide vest length and transfer that measurement (**A**) to two sheets of paper. Take measurement (**B**) for the front and back panel widths; mark each pattern. Slant shoulder as shown, 1½ inches down (fig. 18–2).

2. Mark center of panel and use this line to mark center points on vest front and back. Cut apart front panel along center line.

3. Mark the neckline on front and back panels, then cut away front neckline as shown in figure 18–3.

4. Determine width of side panels by subtracting the combined width of the front and back panels from the bust measurement (**C**) *plus* 2 inches. Divide that number in half since you have two side panels. The remaining figure will be the width of each side panel. Cut a pattern 8 inches high by that measurement, check-

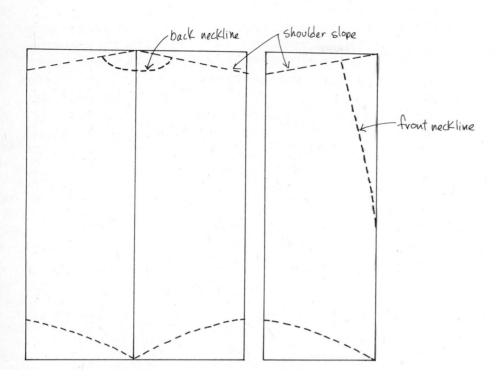

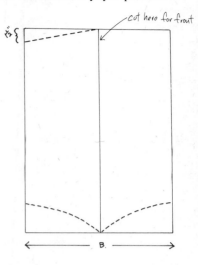

18-2. Make a paper pattern.

18-3. Neckline cuts—take your pick.

ing to make sure that will leave enough room for the shoulder to armhole depth taken earlier. (If you make a shorter vest, waist or bolero length, it sometimes reduces the armhole to uncomfortable proportions. In that case, shorten side panel as necessary for comfort and fit.)

5. Cut front and back panels from commercially quilted velvet and lining fabric.
6. Cut side panels from batting and lining fabric.
7. Cut strips 2 inches wide or wider for string quilting.
8. Review the tips on string quilting in *Beginnings*. Baste or pin batting to backing for side panels. For interest, string quilt pieces on an angle as shown in figure 18-4. Finger press seams as you go; a hot iron would flatten velvet. Baste through fabric all layers around edges of side panels and trim away excess fabric.

18-4. Side panels.

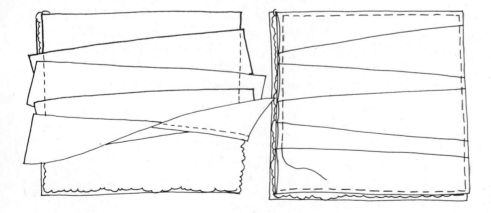

9. Mark a circle on the vest back (a dinner plate makes a good template) with tailor's chalk. Mark a smaller circle inside the larger one (a luncheon plate would work well). This will frame the art nouveau roses.

10. Plan graceful, undulating lines for the stems. Use lighter weight ribbon for the bud stems and velvet cording for the rose stems. Use matching thread to appliqué or blindstitch stems in place.

11. Cut leaves from silk and velvet. Sew together and clip curves as shown in figure 18–5. Turn, stitch opening shut, and press lightly. Tack in place using a blindstitch. Accentuate with French knots made with embroidery thread in harmonizing colors.

18–5. Stem and leaf placement.

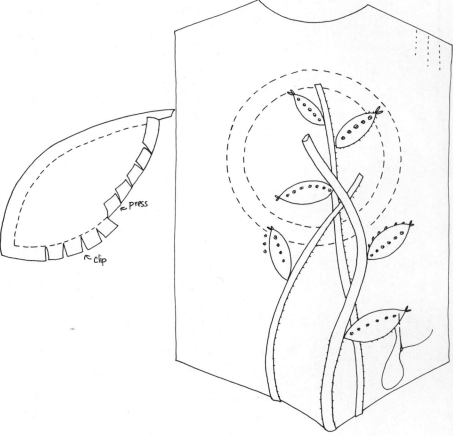

12. Fold ribbon buds as shown and tack folds in place (fig. 18–6). Add different shades of ribbon to give the buds depth and realism, and wrap to resemble folded petals. Tack folds firmly on the back and in areas where the stitches will not show. Sew buds in place on stems, covering the raw end of ribbon. Cut a "calyx" of green silk to cover the bottom of ribbon buds. Appliqué in place, turning under raw edges with the point of your needle as you go.

18–6. Fold buds as shown and stitch in place by hand.

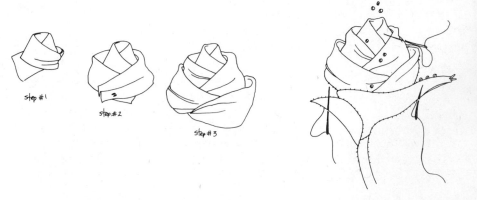

13. Cut two rose petals from lining fabric or silk or taffeta. Appliqué two of them. You might enclose a bit of batting to add dimension to the petal shapes. Gather the bottom of the back petals as you appliqué.

14. Fold and tack the center of the rose as you did the buds. Tack it into place on the two underpetals (fig. 18–7).

15. Cut one large petal from taffeta or silk and experiment with placement over the rose and back petals for best effect. Pin, then appliqué in place. Accent with French knots in shades of pink and mauve (fig. 18–8).

16. Work a double row of pearl beads and knots of metallic thread to delineate the circles. Thread a fine needle with metallic thread and make a French knot, following the outer circle. Take a stitch and pick up a bead on your needle. Stick needle back into the fabric just *behind* the point it came out. Take a stitch; make another knot. Take another stitch; add another bead until the circle is completed. Do the inner circle in the same way. Work a delicate line of feather stitching (one strand of metallic thread on your needle) between the two circles (fig. 18–9).

17. Add a single rose bud, stem, and leaves on one shoulder of the vest front. Work a circle of feather stitching to frame it. (A large iced-tea glass is the right size for the circle template.)

18. Make bias binding from lining fabric (see section on seam finishes in *Beginnings*). This vest uses the same fabric for rose petals, lining, and binding to integrate the design. Cut bias 1½ inches wide.

19. Bind top edge of side panels, enclosing all layers.

20. Sew vest shoulder seams, right sides together. Press open carefully on the wrong side over a Turkish towel to avoid flattening velvet. Sew lining seams in the same fashion.

21. Baste lining to front and back vest panels, wrong sides together, around all edges.

22. With the *wrong* sides together, sew side panels to front and back, lining up along the bottom edge (fig. 18–10).

23. Bind the exposed raw edges of the seam with bias binding from vest front, over the shoulder, to vest back. Sew bias on the top of front and back panels by machine, so it can be finished by hand on the inside.

24. Pin velvet ties in place on vest front as shown in figure 18–11. Tie ends in Chinese ball knots (see fig. 7–5).

25. Bind remaining edges with bias binding, catching ends of ties. Finish bias on the inside with a blindstitch.

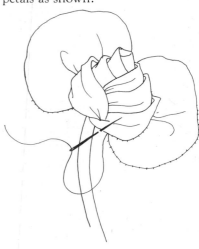

18–7. Sew rose center over two petals as shown.

18–8. Top with third petal. Embellish with French knots.

18–9. Circle detail. See step 16.

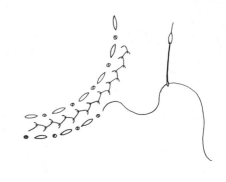

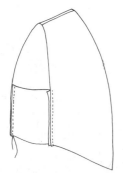

18–10. Sew side panels to vest body.

18–11. Position ties as shown.

VELVET EVENING VEST

The Personal Touch

String quilting on the side panels may be omitted and replaced with the commercially quilted velvet if desired.

Instead of the rose design on the vest back and shoulder, accent the machine quilting with metallic thread in an all-over design. Some fabrics are quilted in a diamond design. If yours is made like that, try accenting stitching lines with metallic thread and sewing a bead at each intersection (fig. 18–12).

Velvet could be hand quilted in an all-over traditional or modern design for a completely handcrafted vest.

Of course, this pattern allows for various shapes—cut bottom edge or neckline to suit your fancy.

18–12. Decorate diamond-quilted fabric or try these basic shape variations.

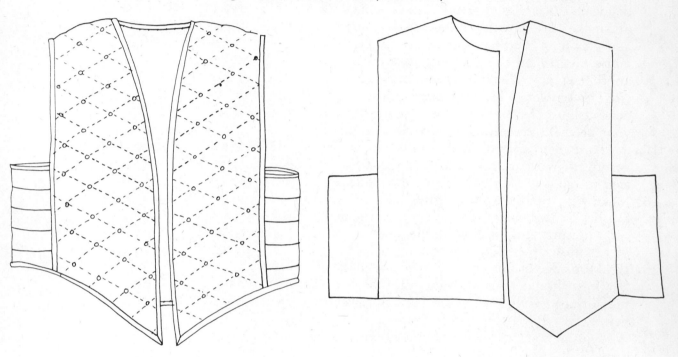

WOMAN'S LACE
AND RIBBON JACKET

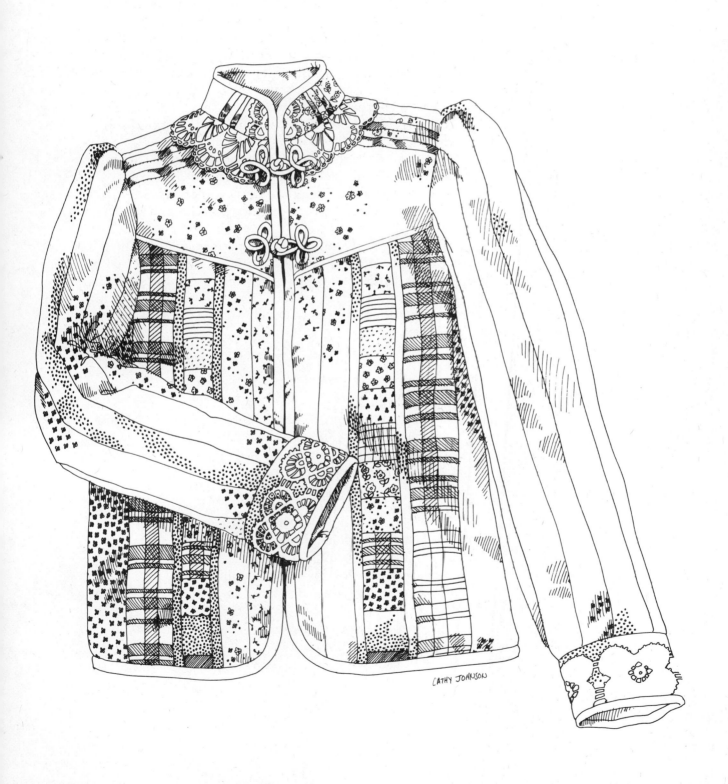

CATHY JOHNSON

Antique doilies have found new life in this garment. Some doilies were stained, some were torn, but all were carefully trimmed or sewn in such a way as to avoid or minimize imperfections, and they now look great! Look carefully at your own old doilies or laces (you can find them in attics, flea markets, antiques stores). Try them out in different ways, and use only parts of doilies if they are badly damaged.

Note: Before using *any* antique textile or lace in your work, make sure it has no historical significance. If it was made by someone who figured in history or if it is a rare or especially well-executed example, it should be preserved as is. Check with an expert if you think you might have something worth keeping, either for historical or artistic reasons. This goes especially for antique quilts. Many old quilts are now being cut up for garments or stuffed toys. If they are old and ragged—*and* of no historical significance—they may find a new lease on life the second time around. Otherwise, preserve them.

How much lace you use depends on what you have available. If you cannot find the curved lace for the stand-up collar, you just will not have it in your jacket. Try to find one especially interesting doily for the back medallion—something round, diamond-shaped, even butterfly-shaped.

You can see in the photo in the color section that it is possible to make a very dressy jacket from old laces and simple fabrics. Since the laces provide all the design interest, you can choose a soft cotton in a neutral color for the background; polycottons will work just as well.

Choose a fairly simple jacket pattern—one without princess seams or bound pockets. I like the puffed sleeves on this one since they seem to complement the slightly old-fashioned air, but any simple pattern can be used. One that takes quilting into account makes fitting easier. The yardages that follow are for a jacket in a woman's size medium.

Materials

- □ pattern for jacket
- □ ¼ yard *each* of eight or nine different fabrics in varying shades
- □ 2½ yards of fabric (for backing)
- □ 2½ yards of fabric (for lining)
- □ 2½ yards of polyester batting
- □ 1 yard of polyester cord (for piping)
- □ ½ yard of fabric for piping
- □ 1 yard *each* of two widths of ribbon
- □ 2 packages of wide bias tape for binding
- □ doilies and lace
- □ scrap of solid fabric for doily medallion
- □ one spool of thread to match lining or harmonize with the overall color
- □ one spool of white or off-white quilting thread
- □ one spool of white thread
- □ two frog closures

1. Make any necessary adjustments to your paper pattern. Plan your yoke design by measuring the desired depth on the paper pattern. Mark and copy on a separate piece of paper or fold back for cutting line. I chose the darkest print for the yoke. The batting and lining will remain a single piece, so you should use the original uncut pattern. Cut out backing, lining, and batting according to your pattern.

2. Pin or baste batting to backing fabric for jacket fronts, backs, and sleeves (see *Beginnings*). Mark the back yoke line with a line of basting stitches.

3. Plan your central medallion for the jacket back. Since this doily has an interesting shape, I made the medallion a chevron shape to echo it. A circle in a square or a diamond-shaped medallion are other possibilities, depending on the shape of doily you decide to use. Following the shape and size of your doily, cut a pattern for the medallion, allowing 1 inch all around. I chose a solid black to show the doily to its best advantage.

4. Baste the doily to the background fabric which you have sandwiched with backing and batting. Tack it carefully into place with matching thread around all major design elements. (Many people prepare their doilies by starching them and pinning them to a board to dry, so the design is fully extended. A hot iron carefully applied gives almost the same effect.) Hand quilt through all layers, ¼ inch out from the edges of the doily as shown in figure 19–1.

5. Position medallion on jacket back and trace medallion outline with tailor's chalk. Cut away batting where your medallion will go to reduce bulk. Fit medallion into the hole and baste in place near the outside edge through all layers. Tack down the edges of the jacket batting so it abuts the medallion batting (fig. 19–2). This will prevent gaps or holes in the jacket's overall padding.

6. Cut strips 2 inches by selvage width from your fabrics and lay them out according to color or shade for easy access. (I planned an ombré effect, shading fabrics from light to dark or dark to light.)

7. Review tips on string quilting in *Beginnings*. String quilt along the edges of the medallion. Sew strips from the point of the chevron (if your medallion is this shape) to the top edge as shown to minimize bunching or puckering (fig. 19–3). Make sure raw edges of the medallion are well covered. Continue until you reach the sides and bottom of the jacket back.

8. Again, mark the yoke over the tops of the strips and the top edge of the medallion (use basting stitches, tailor's chalk, or "invisible" marker). Be sure all raw edges are above this line.

9. Make bias binding 1 inch wide (see section on seam finishes in *Beginnings*). Fold in half lengthwise and enclose polyester cord. Stitch, using a zipper foot to allow you to sew close to the cord.

10. Cut piping to the length of your yoke width. Still using a zipper foot, stitch piping in place, with cord to the bottom and raw edges to the top, as shown in figure 19–4.

11. Lay yoke fabric over the edge of the piping and stitch in place. (Use the zipper foot and hold your fingers lightly over the edge of the fabric and piping to accentuate the raised piping as you feed

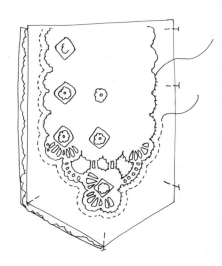

19–1. Construct doily medallion as shown.

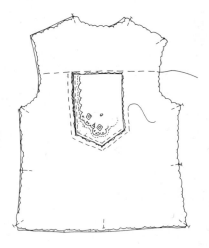

19–2. Baste into place on jacket back.

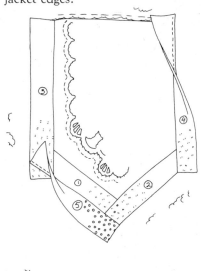

19–3. String quilt as shown to jacket edges.

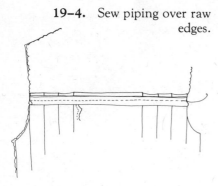

19–4. Sew piping over raw edges.

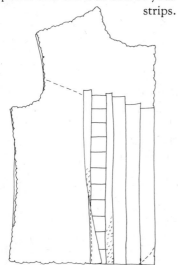

19–5. Construct a "stack" of squares and use it as one of your strips.

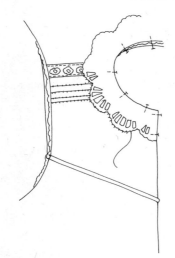

19–6. Add lace to neckline with hand stitching.

the fabric into the sewing machine. This will show you where the edge of the cording is and ensure a close seam.)

12. Fold yoke fabric back over raw edges to the jacket's shoulder line. Pin into place, press, and trim away excess fabric, using backing as a cutting line.

13. Mark yoke on front sections. Begin string quilting at the jacket fronts by securing the first strip flat to the seam line. String quilt three 2-inch strips to each front.

14. Cut four strips, each 1 inch wide, from a darker color. Add one of these strips to each side.

15. Construct the stack by cutting two 2-inch squares of *each* of your fabrics. Sew them together in strips, starting with the lightest and ending with the darkest color. (I incorporated a few fabrics not used in the rest of the jacket to accentuate the shaded effect and to make the strips long enough. These strips are thirteen squares long; the top and bottom squares will be partly hidden under the yoke and binding.)

16. String quilt the stack in place, darkest fabric at bottom. Add the other 1-inch strip (fig. 19–5). Continue string quilting to the sides of the jacket. Be sure the upper edges of the strips extend above the yoke line. Since that edge slants, the strips will need to be progressively longer.

17. Add piping and yoke on jacket fronts as you did in steps 10–12.

18. Stitch jacket fronts and back, right sides together, at shoulder seams. Trim batting and press open. (Do not worry about binding or otherwise finishing seams as the jacket will be lined.)

19. Pin strips of flat lace to right side along seams to form "epaulets." Sew by machine or by hand. Space ribbons on the front yoke, parallel to the edge of the lace. Use two widths and two shades of the same color. Sew in place by hand or machine.

20. I used the lacy curved edge of an old doily to accent the neckline. If you cannot find curved lace, the same effect might be gained by taking darts in purchased lace. Pin lace at neckline, taking care to match lace design in front. Tack down by hand all around the outer edge of major design elements (fig. 19–6).

21. Baste collar fabric (I used second darkest fabric), batting, and backing together. Tack on lace edging to the collar fronts and add ribbon strips as shown in figure 19–7.

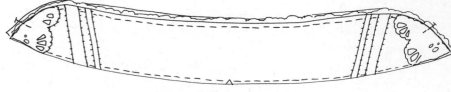

19–7. Collar construction.

22. Attach collar to jacket by matching notches and front edges to front of jacket, with right sides together. Sew through all layers, clip seam curves, and press open.

23. Sew jacket side seams, right sides together. Press open and trim away excess batting and fabric.

24. Mark "cuff" area of sleeves. (They are not true, turned-back cuffs, but contrasting color and trim give that effect.)

25. Beginning in the middle of the sleeve, sew the first strip down

along both edges. (I used my darkest color.) Then add strips along both sides, continuing with lighter colors each time until you reach the edges. Trim away excess fabric, using backing as a guide.

26. Cut a contrasting "cuff" strip to size and string quilt in place, making sure to cover raw edges of sleeve strips at the bottom (fig. 19–8). Turn, press, and trim away excess fabric.
27. Pin lace in place on "cuff" and tack into place.
28. Sew sleeve seams, press open, and trim away excess batting to reduce bulk.
29. The pattern I used called for gathered sleeves, but quilting adds bulk so I chose to make pleats instead. Pleat to fit sleeve opening and pin or baste pleats in place.
30. Set sleeves according to pattern directions.
31. Sew lining seams in the same order—shoulders, collar, sides, sleeve seams, and sleeve inset seams. Press each seam as you go. Do not turn right side out, but work lining into place inside the jacket. Pin at seams and underarm to check fit. Try on the jacket at this point to make sure lining is pinned smoothly in place. Baste all around edges (sleeves, collar, front, bottom).
32. Bind all edges with bias tape. Turn to the inside and stitch by hand.
33. Line up frog closures so the ball button is centered over the front opening. Pin in place and check for proper placement by opening and closing frogs to be sure they work easily. Tack firmly into place, using tiny invisible stitches.

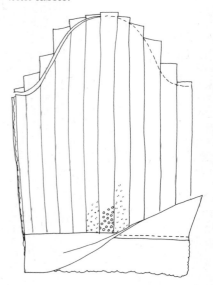

19–8. Cover raw edges of strips with fabric.

Omit lace and use opulent fabrics instead for an oriental feel. Or, for a simpler jacket, choose a backing fabric in a harmonizing color and use it as your lining. Bind seams as in the *Woman's String Quilted Vest*.

Use channel-quilted solid fabrics for the jacket body and lace and doily accents as the major design elements. A dark, rich fabric color will give the best contrast.

A crazy quilt jacket using laces and ribbons in an asymmetrical way would be nice (fig. 19–9).

The Personal Touch

19–9. A crazy quilt jacket.

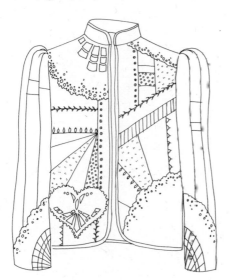

SAMPLER VEST

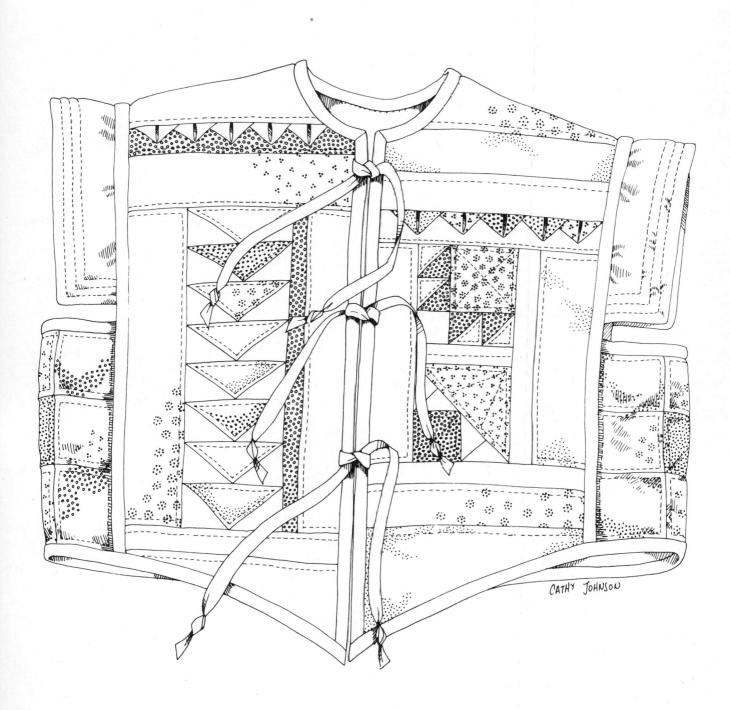

CATHY JOHNSON

For those who are partial to patchwork and hand quilting, here is a vest to satisfy a craving for the traditional and for meditative handwork. Nine Patch, Bear's Paw, Windmill, Flying Geese, and a quarter of the Cross and Crown pattern have all found their way into this bolero-length garment.

As on a pieced bed covering, the amount of hand quilting is up to you. It may be used to accent patchwork squares only or as a design element in each of the string quilted areas. I like a combination of quilted and plain for variation.

Each section is pieced and quilted separately, then lined and joined to make the finished vest. It is a variation of a basic shape designed by Yvonne Porcella, but this version was shortened to bolero length and the stand-up collar was omitted. Since the overall scale was altered, the sleeves were shortened also (see photo in color section).

This is the perfect place to use your own favorite patchwork patterns. Scale them down to garment size using the folded-paper method described below. It might be best to make a mock-up of your squares to make sure your pattern fits the area designated. Or, use the patterns provided with this chapter.

The sampler vest is a good "take-along" project. The vest sections may be pieced at home and taken along to quilt in the hammock or by the fire.

Any simple vest pattern could be used if you prefer not to draft your own. Cottons or polycottons are best for this project, and colors may be as traditional or as contemporary as you like. Tiny polka dots in some of your fabrics will add a subtle "texture" to the vest. The yardages that follow are for a woman's size medium.

Materials

- 1 yard of fabric (for lining)
- 1 yard of fabric (for backing)
- quilting fabrics: ¼ yard *each* of eight or nine different fabrics
- 1 yard of polyester batting
- 1 yard *each* of three colors of grosgrain ribbon
- three packages of wide bias tape, *each* in a different color (to match your three major design colors)
- one spool of thread to match your dominant color
- one spool of off-white quilting thread

Directions

1. To measure and graph your pattern, follow the directions given for the *Velvet Evening Vest*. Cut the pattern to waist length or shorter, remembering to adjust the size of the side panels to allow for comfortable armholes. These are about 6½ inches deep, rather than the normal 8 inches, and could be cut shorter for more wearing ease if desired. Sleeves are 14½ inches long and cut as shown in figure 20–1.

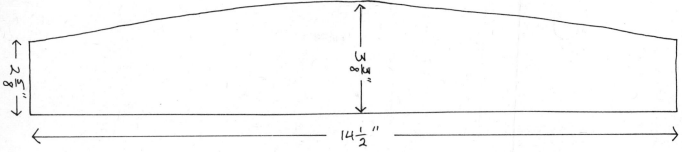

2. Plan the area to be patched on the pattern and cut out paper squares to the size of each patch. Fold each square to your basic design (Four Patch, Nine Patch, etc.) and draw your design on the folded paper as shown in figure 20-2. Then cut apart. Try out sample patches on muslin to be sure everything goes together correctly and is the right size (remember to add ¼-inch seam allowance to all edges). For Prairie Points, cut 2-inch squares from the quilting fabrics and fold and stitch as shown. The background for the patchwork areas are cut as you go along; they fill the remaining space while making a design statement of their own.

20-2. Constructing Prairie Points.

3. Cut your main pattern pieces from backing, lining, and batting. Pin or baste as usual. (Each section of the vest is designed and quilted separately, then the elements are joined to make the whole.)

4. Cut Flying Geese for left front (fig. 20-3). Sew pieces together. The large triangles should have the grain line straight with the longest leg of the triangle. Sew as shown, pressing the first seams away from the large triangle and the connecting seams down. You should have seven "geese" in a line. Pin this strip in place on vest front.

SAMPLER VEST   **131**

20–4. Placement of first patch-work strip.

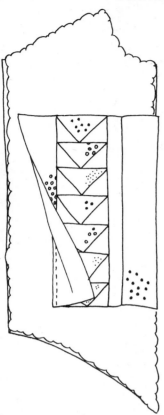

20–3. Flying Geese pattern.

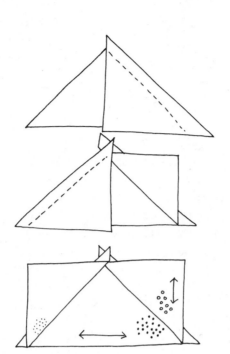

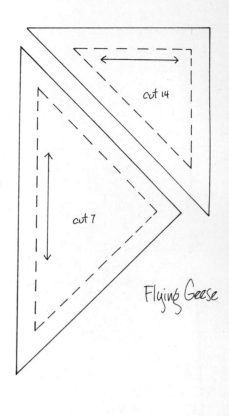

cut 14

cut 7

Flying Geese

20–5. Finishing right front with Prairie Points.

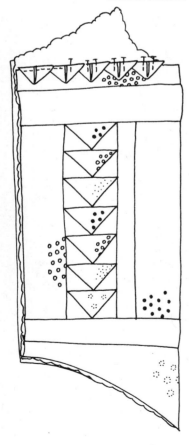

5. Pin Flying Geese strip in place on vest front as shown and cut three strips of varying widths by the length of the finished strip. Review the tips on string quilting in *Beginnings*. String quilt strips in place, as shown in figure 20–4, to cover this section of the vest front.

6. Beginning at the bottom of the section already completed, add more random-width strips till you reach the edge of the garment. Press and trim away excess fabric, using backing as a cutting guide.

7. Do two random-width strips above the completed area, choosing a color to contrast with your Prairie Points. Pin or baste Prairie Points in place as shown in figure 20–5. Experiment with colors to pick up several of those used in the already completed section.

8. Finish string quilting the left side, making sure to enclose the raw upper edges of the Prairie Points with the next strip.

9. Hand quilt as desired (review the tips in *Beginnings*). I quilted inside each of the larger triangles of the Flying Geese and along several of the straight edges, which allowed for a nice contrast of puffy and quilted areas.

10. For right front, cut one quarter section of the Cross and Crown patch (fig. 20–6) and one Bear's Paw patch (fig. 20–7). Stitch together as shown and press seams flat. Cut a strip of fabric 1 inch wide to connect the two patches and sew together as shown in figure 20–8.

11. Pin in place on vest front and string quilt to the garment edges as you did in step 5.

12. Add strips to reach the bottom of the vest; press, pin, and trim away excess.

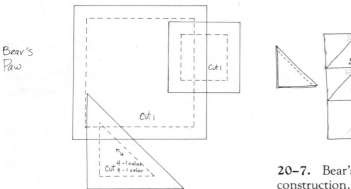

Cross and
Crown

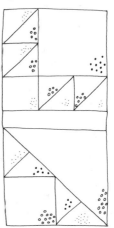

Bear's
Paw

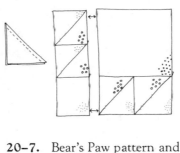

20-7. Bear's Paw pattern and construction.

20-8. Placement of patchwork squares.

13. String quilt a narrow piece above the patchwork area and add Prairie Points (fig. 20-9). (These may be different in color and arrangement from the first strip. I used all my lightest colors against the darkest background on this side.)

14. Continue string quilting to the shoulder line, remembering to vary widths. Trim as usual.

15. Hand quilt to accent your design.

16. The vest back has a variation of the central medallion theme. I used a windmill pattern, but any simple, graphic design would do. Cut the blocks from quilting fabrics and piece together as shown in figure 20-10. Pin in place in the center of the vest back. String quilt to vest bottom with varying fabric widths as shown in figure 20-11. Trim at bottom edge.

17. Frame the block on the sides with string quilting and trim away excess fabric at edges.

18. Add a strip above the quilted area all the way across the vest back and add Prairie Points. (I used alternating solid and polka dot here.)

19. Continue string quilting to the top of the vest back.

20-9. Prairie Points and fabric strips finish left front.

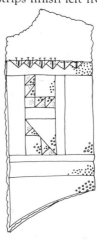

20–11. Stitch onto vest back as shown.

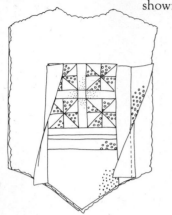

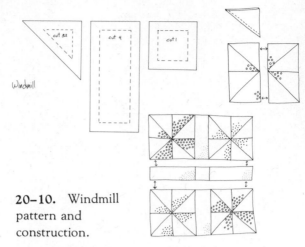

20–10. Windmill pattern and construction.

20. Hand quilt as desired.

21. Cut and piece Nine Patch blocks to fit side panels (one block per panel). Baste all layers together and hand quilt as desired.

22. Baste lining to all quilted pieces, front, back, and side panels.

23. Bind top edge of side panel with bias tape.

24. Layer sleeve sections, right sides together, and place batting on top. Pin or baste, then stitch. Clip corners, turn, and press. Machine quilt with several rows of stitching if desired to help stiffen the sleeves as well as to decorate.

25. Pin vest together at shoulder seams, right sides together. Stitch. Bind inside seams with bias tape.

26. Pin side panels and sleeves to vest, *wrong* sides together. Line up bottom of side panels with the bottom of the vest and center sleeves over the shoulder seams. Stitch in place as shown in figure 20–12. Bind seam on the *outside* of the vest with one color of bias tape.

20–12. Sew side panels to vest body.

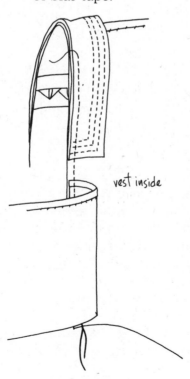

vest inside

27. Cut grosgrain ribbons for ties, six pieces, each ¼ yard long. Knot one end and pin the other into place on vest front.

28. Bind all remaining edges with bias tape. Do not use the color you used to bind the side seams. Be sure to catch ribbon ends under the binding.

You may wish a more symmetrical design, or one that treats the entire vest front as one quilt square. A bed-quilt-sized square could be split in half. You might also cut the neckline a bit lower in back and wear your vest frontwards or backwards (fig. 20–13).

Consider shadow quilting. Make the vest with a layer of bright fabric cut in a pretty design, basted to the batting and backing, and sandwiched under a sheer top fabric. Hand quilt a tulip, scroll, or heart design through all layers with thread to harmonize with the color peeking through.

The Personal Touch

20–13. Variations!

RICH TURKISH COAT

This coat uses the Folkwear Turkish Coat pattern with a number of adaptations. It combines warmth with a really exotic beauty, but if subtle colors are used, it still has great versatility.

The coat pattern itself strives for ethnic authenticity and offers complete directions for hand quilting or trapunto work. This version is Americanized (we need pockets!) *and* simplified considerably. It is made of commercially quilted fabric in a wonderful all-over pattern. Check the back side of the double-faced quilted fabric when you shop; it is often much more interesting than the right side. As you can see in the photo (see color section), the coat was lined with a dark striped fabric to simplify construction and to add protection against the cold.

Like most patterns based on folk or ethnic designs, this coat is made up of simple, flat pieces of cloth with very little complicated fitting or tailoring required. It has a grace and integrity of its own, not dependent on changing fashion or designer cut.

You will find the address for Folkwear, Inc., in the *Where to Buy It* section of this book. When you shop for fabric, look for stripes and small-print fabrics in warm, soft colors. Jinny Beyer's striped border fabric designs for V.I.P. Fabrics are wonderfully exotic, and Liberty prints are always appropriate. The yardages that follow are for a coat in a woman's size medium.

Materials

- ⊔ Folkwear Turkish Coat, pattern 106
- ⊔ 3½ yards of commercially quilted fabric (for coat)
- ⊔ 2 yards of exotic striped fabric (for borders)
- ⊔ 3½ yards of striped fabric (for lining)
- ⊔ ¼ yard *each* of four or five different small-print fabrics
- ⊔ ½ yard of polyester batting
- ⊔ 1 yard of cord (for ties) (optional)
- ⊔ ½ yard *each* of two understated striped ribbons
- ⊔ one large spool of thread to match color of quilted fabric
- ⊔ one spool of thread to match color of lining
- ⊔ one package of piping in a contrasting color

Directions

1. Lay out your pattern and plan fit carefully. The original pattern calls for a length of 51 inches, much longer than needed for optimum versatility, though great for drama. It would keep your ankles warm, too, but as I wanted to keep the coat in scale with my height (5′3″), I shortened all pattern pieces by 8 inches.
2. Tape pattern shoulders together and cut main body section as one large piece. Cut out main body pieces from quilted material, following cutting guide provided with the pattern. Do not cut borders yet.
3. Using these same pattern pieces, cut out lining. If you plan to add pockets, make a pattern and cut four from lining fabric.
4. Cut some of the stripes from the border fabric to use in the yoke area. Allow ¼-inch seam allowances on each side of the printed stripe.

5. Cut strips of varying widths from the dotted material.
6. Sew your pocket pieces to the seam allowances of the quilted-

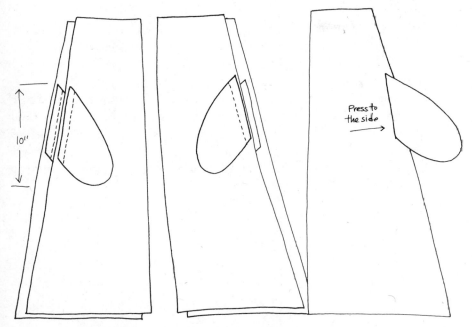

21–1. Cut pockets and sew as shown.

21–2. Sew side seams.

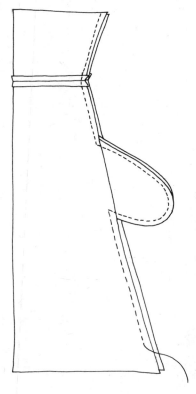

fabric side panels as shown in figure 21–1. Press seam toward pocket.
7. Sew gussets to side panels, then sew the resulting side sections together. Follow the curve of the added pockets as shown in figure 21–2. Press seam to one side. It is not necessary to finish seams in any way since the coat will be lined.
8. To make decorative pocket slits, measure pocket depth on the outside of the coat. Cut four strips from the border fabric to that length plus 4 inches and sew them together. Turn under ends diagonally as shown in figure 21–3, then square off ends. Press edges under. To make machine application easier, turn over side section and roll pocket into a tight roll at the seam. Pin to keep out of the way. Turn to the right side and pin decorative placket in place. Edgestitch all around, then unpin pocket. Slipstitch inner edges to pocket slit by hand.

21–3. Pocket decoration construction.

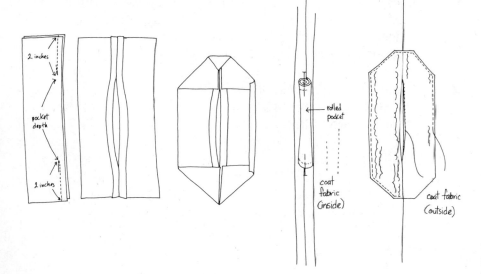

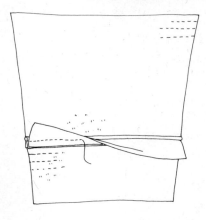

21-4. Sleeve trim.

21-5. Decorative sleeve strip.

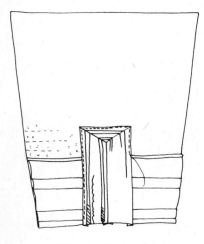

21-6. Strip placement.

21-7. Batting placement and trim.

9. Plan depth of sleeve decoration. Mark with tailor's chalk or basting stitches. Using a zipper foot, sew piping along this line with raw edges toward bottom of sleeve. (Review tips on string quilting in *Beginnings*.)

10. Lay a strip of fabric along the piping as shown in figure 21-4 and stitch (still using zipper foot) close to the raised edge. Turn and press. Continue string quilting until you reach the bottom of the sleeve edge, using varying widths of fabric.

11. Cut one of the border stripes approximately 20 inches long. Fold one edge (along the design of the stripe) ¼ inch to wrong side and press. Fold fabric in half and stitch as shown along the other edge of the stripe. Clip corner and turn fabric so there is a sharp point. Open out flat. Fold point down to meet center seam and press. Slipstitch in place (fig. 21-5).

12. Position this over the center of the sleeve as shown in figure 21-6. Pin and edgestitch in place. Sew sleeve seams to dot on pattern and press open.

13. Plan yoke area on the coat body and cut a piece of batting to fit. This will add extra warmth in the shoulders and upper back as well as add to the puffy, quilted effect (most commercially quilted fabrics use a very lightweight batting). Baste the batting in place. Cut a strip of border fabric and fold into a chevron shape; turn under raw edges and edgestitch in place on coat back.

14. Beginning at the bottom of the batting, sew a length of piping in place (use zipper foot). Be sure to cover the raw edge at the top of the chevron stripe (fig. 21-7).

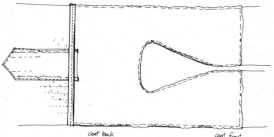

coat back   coat front

15. String quilt a strip of fabric to the piping as you did in step 10.
16. Sew piping along the bottom edge of the yoke on coat fronts (use zipper foot).
17. String quilt up from the back and over the shoulders to the front of the coat. Trim the border-striped fabric and use whatever part of the design you like (to give a variety). Include a strip of lining fabric to provide continuity in the design.
18. Continue string quilting until you reach the piping. Carefully fold the raw edge of the last strip so it covers the stitching on the piping and press in place. Pin and stitch as close to the piping as possible (fig. 21-8).
19. Edgestitch ribbon in place over seams wherever it is most effective in terms of color or pattern.
20. Trim away excess fabric around neckline and shoulders, using coat fabric as a cutting line.
21. If desired, cut two squares from your border-striped fabric. Cut squares diagonally as shown and piece together as shown to form border medallion. Turn under edges and appliqué in place on one yoke front (fig. 21-9).

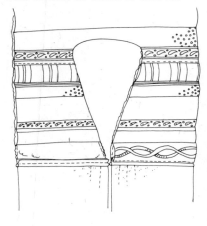

21-8. String-quilted yoke. Trim with ribbon or braid as desired.

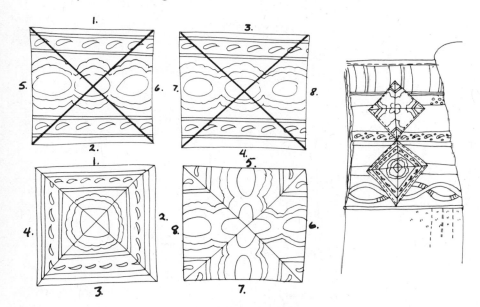

21-9. Medallions for yoke.

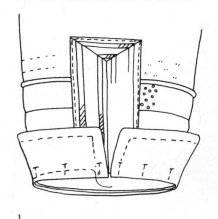

21-10. Attach cuffs as shown.

22. Add extensions to coat fronts and press seam open.
23. Cut sleeve cuff from border fabric, checking the lengthwise measurement if you have changed the length of the sleeve. (Other fabric can be substituted if desired.) Cut top, backing, and batting. If you plan to use your body fabric as backing, just cut two of the border stripe and two of body fabric. Layer fabric, right sides together, with batting on top. Sew together, clip corners, and turn. Press and machine or hand quilt if desired.
24. The pattern called for lining up the cuff opening with the underarm seam, but I wanted it to continue the sleeve decoration. Part of the joy of creating handmade garments is designing as you go along, and in this case it was a good decision. Pin cuff to sleeve as shown in figure 21-10, with cuff opening centered under the decorative placket. Stitch and press seam up into sleeve.
25. Fit sleeve into place at the top of the side panel as shown in the pattern directions, matching dots.

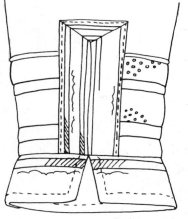

26. Pin body of coat to side panels, right sides together. Stitch and press seams toward the middle of the body. Cover this seam on the outside with decorative braid, ribbon, or border-striped fabric strips. It is best to sew it on by hand, since the seam follows the shoulder curve.

27. When coat body is all assembled, check the measurements for the borders as suggested in the pattern directions. If you are using a border-striped fabric, I would suggest altering the directions slightly so the front borders extend all the way to the bottom of the coat as shown in figure 21–11, instead of as the pattern directions suggest. Otherwise, follow their directions for cutting. You may use your body fabric as backing for the borders as I did, or cut batting and backing. Clip corners, turn, and press. Hand or machine quilt back border as desired.

21–11. Front and back border construction.

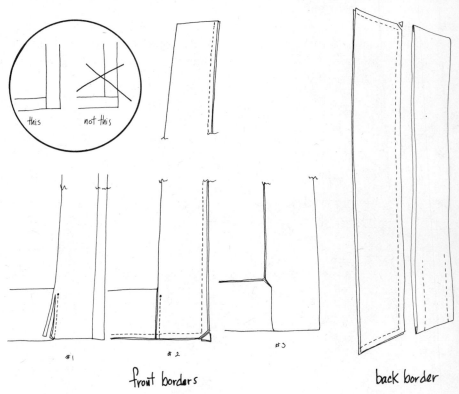

front borders   back border

28. Fit back section of border in place as shown in figure 21–12. Sew in place.

21–12. Sew back border as shown.

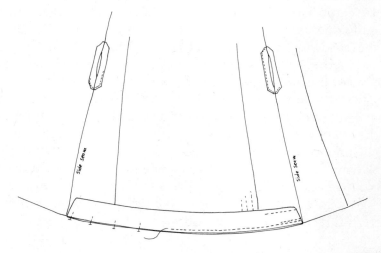

29. Pin ties in place on front.

30. You will have sewn the side edge of the bottom front border section when you sewed the other seams (Folkwear's directions did not make this clear). Line it up with the side seams and the back border as shown in figure 21–13, and stitch to the front edge of the coat.

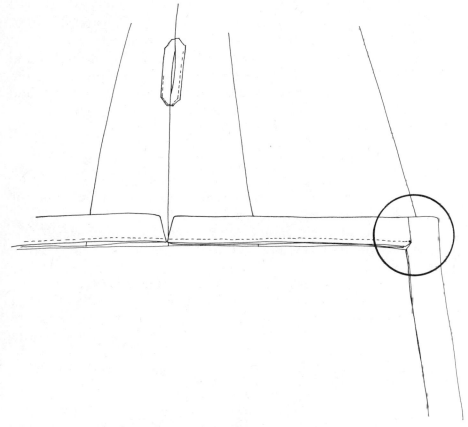

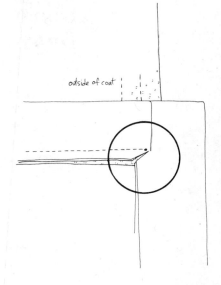

21–13. Front border sewn in place on coat bottom.

21–14. Clip as shown.

outside of coat

31. Clip corner of border only, as shown in figure 21–14.

32. Turn border so the raw edges are along the raw edge of the coat front as shown in figure 21–15. Check the corner on the right side of the coat for a smooth fit before sewing. Stitch to within 12 inches of the back neck on both sides.

21–15. Turn and stitch to coat front.

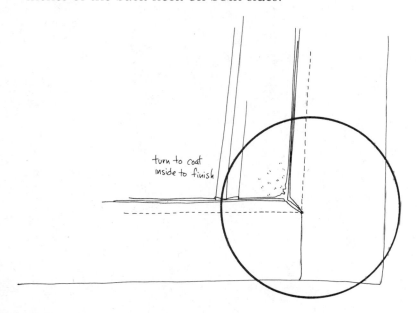

turn to coat
inside to finish

33. Check fit of border by pinning it to meet at the center back of the coat. Trim away excess fabric if necessary. Pin seam at border center to fit and sew, taking a ½-inch seam. Fold to enclose seam and continue stitching border in place. (See Folkwear pattern directions.)
34. Machine or hand quilt as desired.
35. Sew lining together as you did coat body, but omit borders. Turn under raw edges all around and press. Press border edges and raw edges of sleeve toward inside of coat.
36. Fit the lining into the coat, matching underarm seams and gussets. Pin at those points for correct fit, then proceed to pin lining to the edges of the coat body, covering all raw edges. Hand stitch in place with a good, firm stitch.

The Personal Touch

Instead of buying quilted fabric, sandwich batting between two layers of fabric and hand quilt the entire coat. And consider Folkwear's directions for a trapunto border—it's a knockout.

This would be a magnificent evening coat made with shadow-quilting. White with a golden scroll and quilted borders would be very elegant.

One tends to think of the Turkish Coat as a warm winter project only, but the basic shape makes a great summer robe. Cut one layer of fabric only, and finish the edges with machine zigzag on the inside. Bind edges with a simple kimono-style band of contrasting fabric.

This garment also works as a short jacket. Add a tie belt if you like!

21–16. A shadow-quilted coat and bathrobe variations.

Designers' Scrapbook

We are no longer a people who slavishly follow the dictates of fashion—if indeed we ever were. Couturiers still work in Paris and Milan and New York, and we are influenced by their ideas, to be sure. But designers are popping up everywhere: Modesto, California; Sisters, Oregon; Overland Park and Lawrence in Kansas; Excelsior Springs, Missouri; Indiana; Mississippi; Colorado—we have become our own designers, and we have discovered the joy and freedom it brings us.

The sixties set us free to express ourselves in our body coverings, and our designs have matured in the intervening years. No longer do handmade garments look "weird" or "hippie," but classic and beautiful.

Ideas are everywhere, as designers are everywhere. Our environment influences us; our needs change us; our problems blossom into creativity.

These are a few of the designers at work today, creating for themselves, for friends, for a livelihood. Look and enjoy. In their diversity of style and color and preference, I hope these designers serve to inspire you to try your *own* designs, to branch out, to trust your wings and fly.

Donna Adam lives and works in Kansas City, in a beautiful old home near the Plaza. Her studio is a wonder of organization, a *working* work-of-art. A prolific designer, Donna has owned her own crafts gallery and now has turned her attention to supplying galleries and shops instead of running one. Donna enjoys string quilting with a twist— old lace, hand embroidery, sumptuous fabrics.

Her wool and satin vest (third from the left) is wonderful for winter evenings, while the blue-bordered vest (second from the left) looks like summer. Donna's vests demonstrate her remarkable versatility within the discipline of strip quilting. Her Polska Vest (second from the right) features a wide color range.

Roberta Hammer of Excelsior Springs, Missouri, designs mostly for children (see *Rachel's Machine-appliquéd Vest*), and the wonderful clothes worn by her five children provide plenty of inspiration for others. Nora's Quilted Baby Coat, shown here, is delicate in color, but goes beyond the usual baby-sweetness. Hand-appliquéd hearts top quilted scallops and a tiny-plaid lining adds a bit of piquancy.

Yvonne Porcella of Modesto, California, has made a name for herself with her bold ethnic shapes and intricate piecing, as well as for knock-'em-dead colors. This coat is ample demonstration of all of the above! Yvonne has published several books on pieced or ethnic garments (see *Sourcebooks*). Several of the projects in this book were based (loosely, in some cases!) on her cutting and measuring directions, which are clear and easy to follow.

Old quilts that have outlived their usefulness are the inspiration for Rosanna Anderson of Smithville, Missouri. Rosanna uses "only those quilts too far gone" to repair or use for her vests, and carefully plans pattern placement to make the most of the quilts she finds at flea markets, garage sales, and auctions.

Sisters, Oregon, is home for Jean Wells, where she designs, teaches, and runs a shop. Her clothes provide inspiration for all who love old lace and pretty doilies and who appreciate fine use of color. Jean is the author of *A Patchworthy Apparel Book*. This jacket shows just why Jean is well known in handcrafting circles.

At the Square Patch in Richmond, Missouri, Bettie Blair works quietly away at some of the finest hand work I have yet seen. The vest shown at the bottom of this photo was first photographed, inadvertently, wrong side out. Her stitches were so fine I could not tell the difference. Close inspection revealed a dainty scalloped edge—it was the stitching line of the binding! Bettie also interpreted the Tulip-Patch vest (top) from a design by Ellen Mosbarger.

Also from the Square Patch, in Richmond, Missouri, Louise Reyburn made this Fan Vest from a design by Eleanor Nelson, a Kansas resident who calls Overland Park home. Eleanor says she plans to have the pattern available for this pretty, nostalgic vest.

This sundress of Seminole patchwork proves that all work of this kind need not be on cool-weather clothes.

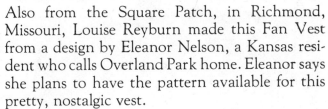

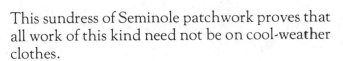

Our scrapbook also includes several of my own designs that were not included in the projects section. Harris's Machine-appliquéd Shirt, right, is as cheerful as daybreak—or is that sunset on that yoke? The Western Shirt on the left makes use of patchwork for cuffs, collar, and yoke and unbleached muslin for the body.

The White-on-White Vest made use of part of my large—and growing—collection of old laces, doilies, and linens. The antimacassars of yesterday have become the decorations of today.

Metric Conversions

Inches	Millimeters	Inches	Millimeters
1/32	.7938	17/32	13.4938
1/16	1.5875	9/16	14.2875
3/32	2.3813	19/32	15.0813
1/8	3.175	5/8	15.875
5/32	3.9688	21/32	16.6688
3/16	4.7625	11/16	17.4625
7/32	5.5563	23/32	18.2563
1/4	6.35	3/4	19.05
9/32	7.1438	25/32	19.8438
5/16	7.9375	13/16	20.6375
11/32	8.7313	27/32	21.4313
3/8	9.525	7/8	22.225
13/32	10.3188	29/32	23.0188
7/16	11.1125	15/16	23.8125
15/32	11.9063	31/32	24.6063
1/2	12.70	1	25.4001

1 foot = 0.304 meters
1 yard = 0.914 meters
1 square inch = 64.52 square mm
1 square foot = 9290.3 square mm
1 square yard = 0.836 square m

Where to Buy It

Patterns

Folkwear, Inc., Box 3798, San Rafael, California 94902

    Folkwear makes patterns for ethnic and antique clothes, timeless and elegant. The instructions are all hand-written—charming but occasionally a little hard to understand. Well worth the effort, though. Nice people, too.

Fashion Blueprints, P.O. Box 21141, Minneapolis, Minnesota 55421

    Interesting, simple clothes with classic, ethnic styling.

Past Patterns, 2017 Eastern S.E., Grand Rapids, Michigan 49507

    Beautiful reproductions of antique styles, easily adaptable to today's uses.

Simplicity, *McCall's*, *Butterick*, and *Vogue* patterns are all worth using. See your local fabric stores.

Kits

Many of the kits available by mail and in specialty stores can be personalized to suit your taste: Seminole patchwork, machine appliqué, hand-pieced squares, etc. These companies carry vests, coats, and jackets as well as accessories that lend themselves to interpretation quite willingly.

Country Ways, Inc., 221 Winter Street, Excelsior, Minnesota 55331

    These are very helpful folks. Their pattern directions are clearly written and well illustrated.

Frostline Kits, Frostline Circle, Denver, Colorado 80241

    Beautiful, well-cut clothes.

Mail Order Fabrics

Brewer Fabric Shop, Twin City Plaza, Brewer, Maine 04412

    Send $3.50 for 800 fabric swatches. They have calicoes, solids, chintzes, and border prints.

Calico 'N Things, P.O. Box 265, Marquette, Michigan 49855

    Try them for quilting supplies and fabrics.

Country Heirlooms, Village Shopping Center, Hope, Arkansas 71801

    Write for mail order catalog, $1.00. They have pin dots, Jinny Beyer Fabrics, and calicoes.

Jehlor Fantasy Fabrics, The Pavilion Outlet Center, 17900 Southcenter Parkway, Seattle, Washington 98188

    For specialty fabrics and trims.

Pelikow, Box 225, Beverly, New Jersey 08010

    For velveteen remnants by the pound.

Scheepjeswol USA, Inc., 155 Lafayette Avenue, North White Plains, New York 10603 *or Scheepjeswol (Canada) Ltd.*, 400 B Montee de Liesse, Montreal, Quebec H4T IN8

    For beautiful fabrics and yarns. They have a line of dutch cottons that would be wonderful for the Turkish Coat.

Utex Trading, 710 Ninth Street, Suite S, Niagara Falls, New York 14301

    Try them for silks imported from China, Fuji, and Thailand; jacquards, taffetas, and shantungs.

Sourcebooks

As someone who sews and quilts, I am always on the lookout for inspiration and new ideas. A great place to look is in books. Sometimes I find a quilt block that I never knew existed; other times I come across a fantastic idea for a quilted garment. And there is always the hope I will chance upon a shortcut that will make my life easier.

    These are some of the books I have found helpful and inspiring.

General

Quilting, by Averil Colby (New York: Scribner's, 1971), and Florence Peto's *Historic Quilts* (New York: The American Historical Co., 1939) are both recommended by the National Museum of American History. *Quilting* is a comprehensive guide to traditional quilting. It contains some amazing photos of early quilted clothing that should be an inspiration and a challenge to the designer.

Yours Truly, Inc., has published a vast array of Seminole designs with Cheryl Greider Bradkin's *The Seminole Patchwork Book*. This book is well illustrated, easily understood, and belongs in your library. (Write to Yours Truly, Inc., Box 80218, Atlanta, Georgia 30366.) Marjorie Puckett explores the subject of shadow quilting in *Lighter Shade of Pale*, published by Orange Patchwork Publishers (P.O. Box 2557, Orange, California 92669).

One of the best books on straight sewing that I've ever seen is *Sew Smart* by Judy Lawrence and Clotilde Yurick. It includes couturiers' tricks of the trade and shortcuts that do not end up looking like shortcuts. It is available at fine fabric stores or write to Sewing Kits, Inc., P.O. Box 1493, Boulder, Colorado 80306.

Patchwork

A classic collection of patchwork patterns is Ruby McKim's *One Hundred and One Patchwork Patterns*, published in New York (1962) by Dover Books. It is a good place to look for patterns to use on a vest or a jacket, and most of the patterns have templates. Or, for an interesting variation on my clothing ideas, try a medallion jacket using one of the fifty quilt blocks from *The United States Patchwork Pattern Book* by Barbara Bannister and Edna Paris Ford. This is another of the many craft books published by Dover (1976), and templates are included for all fifty designs.

The next two books are wonderful idea starters. Jinny Beyer's *Patchwork Patterns* (published by EPM Productions, Inc., 1003 Turkey Run Road, McLean, Virginia 22101) will help you utilize any quilt pattern you like in the size you need. It also shows how to design your own patterns. *Hearts & Tulips*, by Chris Wolf Edmonds, is a collection of charming patchwork patterns. The drawings by Marina Wood suggest clothing adaptations. This book is put out by Yours Truly, Inc., P.O. Box 80218, Atlanta, Georgia 30366.

Clothing

Marjorie Puckett has written two good "idea catalyst" books: *String Quilts and Things* and *Flowers are Forever*. You should check these books out! Both are published by Orange Patchwork Publishers, P.O. Box 2557, Orange, California 92669. Another great source is Jean Ray Laury's *Quilted Clothing* (Oxmoor House, Inc., P.O. Box 2463, Birmingham, Alabama 35201). Laury gives designs for quilted vests, coats, jackets, and a number of other handcrafted—but nonquilted—designs.

Quilts to Wear, by Virginia Avery (New York: Scribner's, 1982), contains some very elegant designs. Especially noteworthy is the Samurai Vest. And for delightful use of old laces and doilies, see *A Patchworthy Apparel Book*. In it, Jean Wells has included a wonderful collection of clothes of all kinds (Yours Truly, Inc., P.O. Box 80218, Atlanta, Georgia, 30366).

For books full of garments with beautiful ethnic styling coupled with an intricate piecing method and an incredible sense of color, see Yvonne Porcella's three books: *Five Ethnic Patterns*, *Pieced Clothing*, and *Pieced Clothing Variations*. All books include patterns and cutting instructions and are available through Porcella Studios, 3619 Shoemaker Avenue, Modesto, California 95351.

Many of the ethnic patterns in *Ethnic Costume*, by Diane Ericson and Lois Ericson (New York: Van Nostrand Reinhold, 1979), would lend themselves to your own quilted interpretations. Also valuable is Dorothy K. Burnham's *Cut My Cote*, available through the Textile Department, Royal Ontario Museum, Toronto, Canada (ROM 972.248.1). This is a collection of ethnic clothing from the Royal Ontario Museum, and it includes cutting layouts and sewing instructions for garments from Rumanian shirts to Greek dresses, from Korean coats to Japanese kimonos.

And for the last word in shoes, look at George M. White's *Craft Manual of North American Footwear* (published by the author, P.O. Box 365, Ronan, Montana 59864). I used one of White's designs as the basis for my Warm Winter Slippers pattern in *Quiltwear*. Many of his other ideas look promising.

INDEX